# AROUND
## THE WORLD IN
# 80 RAVES

# AROUND
## THE WORLD IN
# 80 RAVES

A guide to the best parties
and festivals on the planet

**MARCUS BARNES**

DOG 'n' BONE

# Acknowledgments

Thanks to everyone who has helped in the making of this book. Without the aid of countless PRs, photographers, and festival promoters, the project would never have been possible. I also owe a huge debt to my good, good friend Emma, and would like to dedicate this book to my partner Marion, my Nan, Mum, sister Karina, nephew Amari and all my wonderful friends around the world.

Published in 2013 by Dog 'n' Bone Books
An imprint of Ryland Peters & Small Ltd

20–21 Jockey's Fields     519 Broadway,
London WC1R 4BW          5th Floor
                         New York, NY 10012

www.rylandpeters.com

10 9 8 7 6 5 4 3 2

Text © Marcus Barnes 2013
Design © Dog 'n' Bone Books 2013

ISBN: 978 1 909313 12 5

Printed in China

Editor: Pete Jorgensen
Designer: Mark Latter
Picture credits: 2 iStock; 4 Katy Davies/Creamfields; 6 Isle of Wight Festival; 8 and 11 Bestival; 12–13 Bugged Out; 15 bottom Heal Houghton/Creamfields; 15 top Anthony Mooney; 17 Marc Sethi/Eastern Electrics; 18 Farr Festival; 19 We Are FSTVL; 21 Field Day; 23 iStock; 26 iStock; 27 iStock; 28 Isle of Wight Festival; 29 Latitude; 30 and 31 Leeds & Reading; 33 Lovebox; 34 and 35 Parklife; 36 and 37 iStock; 39 iStock; 40 T In The Park; 41 Wilderness; 43 V Festival; 44 Hideout; 47 10 Days Off; 49 iStock; 50 and 51 bottom 01studio.eu/Audioriver; 51 top Cezary Dziecielski/Audioriver; 52 Istvan Bielik/Balaton Sound; 53 FIB File/ Liberto Peiro; 54 Stephan Flad/Berlin Festival; 55 Boom Festival; 56 Dimensions; 57 Dour Festival 2012 – Grooveman; 58 Exit Festival; 60 The Garden Festival; 62 and 63 Hideout; 64 I Love Techno; 65 iStock; 66 Love System Festival; 67 Stephan Flad/Melt!; 68 Motel Mozaique; 70 Joao Bacelar/Optimus Alive; 71 Outlook; 72 Øya; 73 Positivus; 74 Dani Canto/ Primavera Sound; 75 Joris Bulckens/ Pukkelpop; 76 and 77 Rock En Seine; 78 Lars Just/POLFOTO/Roskilde Festival; 79 Vegard S. Kristiansen/Roskilde Festival; 82 bottom Edwin Van Der Heide/Sonar; 82 top Sonar; 83 Stop Making Sense; 84 Tomorrowland; 85 Anna Spysz/Unsound; 86 Unknown; 87 Heather Shuker; 88 Weather Festival; 89 Pierre Nocca/Worldwide; 90 Miguel Legault/ Igloofest; 92 iStock; 93 Film Magic/Bonnaroo; 94–97 Amos Nelson; 98 and 99 iStock; 100 Rukes/Electric Daisy Carnival; 100 top Jack Edinger/Lollapalooza; 100 bottom Ashley Garman/Lollapalooza; 103 Elise Apap/ Igloofest; 104 Jean Francois Leblanc/Montreal Jazz Festival; 106 Frederique Menard-Aubin/ Montreal Jazz Festival; 106 Movement Detroit; 108 iStock; 109 Woodsist; 110 Sofia Salazar/ SXSW; 110 top Extreme Airshots/SXSW; 110 bottom Otto Helweg/SXSW; 113 Arielle Castillo; 114 Douglas van Sant for TheBPMfestival.com; 116 Virginie Harel/ Afrikaburn; 117 Scott Kowalchyk for TheBPMfestival.com; 118 iStock; 119 Inti Fest; 121 iStock; 123 iStock; 124 iStock; 125 Rukes/www.soundwavefestival.com; 126 Together; 127 Zouk Management see page 128

For digital editions, visit
www.cicobooks.com/apps.php

# CONTENTS

# Introduction

Rave culture is now an integral part of many people's lives, from the teen clubbers of the world to the more discerning boutique festival goers. What started in the late eighties as the offspring of electro, disco, hip hop, and numerous other forms of music, soon permeated into global culture, from acid house parties held in the British countryside to techno raves in darkened warehouses in Berlin. Raving has become embedded in the lifestyles of many people around the globe and there is no better evidence of this than the huge global economy that has built up around big music events, or festivals.

Of course, festivals have been existence for centuries: religious festivals, sun-worshipping festivals, pagan festivals, Christmas, Diwali, and so on—in layman's terms a festival is just an extended celebration of anything. In the modern sense of the word, a festival is typically a music-orientated event with multiple stages, usually with huge production values and all-star line-ups of superstars from all over the world. They have become a staple of many people's lives, from diehard music enthusiasts to those who just want to have a big blow out once in a while. They they are big business, too. Every year hundreds of new festivals pop up from Japan to Canada, Iceland, Australia, and everywhere in between. Raving in fields is still just as prevalent as it was back in the late eighties, it's just that now it's become legitimate and accepted by the mainstream media. With so much choice, and an ever-growing list of festivals to consider, I thought it would be handy to put together a guide to some of the world's best events, complete with basic budget information so you can work out how much you'll spend at each: one star means it's exceptionally cheap, while five stars means you're going to have to splash out. Each festival has its own nuances, its own "vibe" and ethos, and each is a new adventure to embark on with your friends and loved ones... So join me as we go Around The World In 80 Raves...

# Chapter 1

## United Kingdom

# Bestival

## ISLE OF WIGHT, ENGLAND

The Isle of Wight plays host to two big festivals every year, one which is named after the island itself and features a more rock- and pop-based selection of musicians, and one which is a crazy kaleidoscope of colors, sounds, and experiences. Bestival is the name of the latter and it's pretty much a huge playground for adults. If you can think back to being a kid and how you imagined life as a grown-up — being able to run around and play whenever you want with no one to tell you off — then Bestival is basically that! Held in Robin Hill Country Park, the party closes Britain's festival season every September, being one of the last of the famous gatherings that take place across the nation during the summer months.

**DATE:** FIRST WEEKEND IN SEPTEMBER

**PAST HEADLINERS:** SNOOP DOGG, BEASTIE BOYS, FLAMING LIPS, ELTON JOHN, THE CURE, THE CHEMICAL BROTHERS, BJÖRK, FLORENCE AND THE MACHINE

**TICKET PRICE:** ✪✪✪✪

**ACCOMMODATION:** ✪✪✪

**PRICE OF BEER:** ✪✪✪✪

**PRICE OF CIGARETTES:** ✪✪✪✪

**AVERAGE COST OF A SNACK AT THE FESTIVAL:** ✪✪✪

There are various factors that contribute to the beauty of Bestival, from the groups of open-minded people of all ages and walks of life who attend every year to the excellent line-ups where you can find pretty much every kind of music you can imagine, from folk and reggae to blues and psy-trance. Then there are the little touches that make the Bestival experience so special, like the ever-popular fancy dress themes, the attention to detail evident in the highly decorated tents, the focus on being environmentally friendly, and the secret areas that you accidently stumble across. The phrase "there's something for everyone" is clichéd for a reason, but it's actually pretty apt for Bestival. If you're a fitness nut the organizers offer the chance to swim to the festival for charity, or if you fancy commemorating your visit by getting a tattoo, you can pay a visit to Sailor Jerry's parlor.

It's a huge annual event, so attracts plenty of visitors from across the UK, as well as the up-for-it locals, giving the festival a really great mix of people. Besides the usual teen festival fanatics, it's not uncommon to see families popping in to witness the smorgasbord of spectacular sights on offer—from the main stage where acts like Public Enemy, Magnetic Man, and Kelis have performed, through to the smaller stages and tents where bands and DJs like David Rodigan, Hot Chip, Primal Scream, Fat Boy Slim, Belle & Sebastian, and Shy FX can be found.

The 2013 edition marked the 10th anniversary of Bestival with a special navy theme to tie proceedings together. The festival's much-loved organizer, Rob Da Bank, can now be found at the helm leading his merry crew into uncharted waters for what hopefully will be another 10 years of fun and games. Whatever age you are, Bestival is bound to bring out your inner child. Just a few minutes in the infamous Wishing Tree will see to that!

# Bugged Out Weekender

## BOGNOR REGIS, ENGLAND

When I was a child my Grandad (RIP) took my cousins and I to Bognor Regis on many, many occasions, which is why the seaside town has a special place in my heart. Over 25 years later it's still somewhere that I consider to be worth a visit for a bit of fun. Now, though, that fun is a little different, involving a little less time spent playing arcade games or throwing pebbles into the sea, and a little more time spent getting wrecked with my mates as we dance away to Aphex Twin (can you dance to Aphex Twin?!) or hold another all-day after-party at our chalet.

Bugged Out Weekender has become a huge feature on the annual festival calendar in the UK, thanks to its gargantuan line-ups and the involvement of many of the nation's finest promoting outfits and club brands. The action all takes place in January, well before the start of the UK's festival season—which means there is very little competition for bookings. To list all the electronic music superstars who have appeared at Bugged Out would take up most of this book, but the mere mention of names like Aphex Twin, The Chemical Brothers, Andrew Weatherall, and Frankie Knuckles should tell you all you need to know about the caliber of performers that they bring in every year.

Yeah, the average age of those in attendance might be a little young for more "experienced" (not old!) ravers like myself, but if you're in your late teens or early twenties... or even in your twenties full stop, then you'll be right at home. Oldies like me, not so much!

> **DATE:** MID-JANUARY
>
> **PAST HEADLINERS:** SCUBA, SCREAM, EROL ALKAN, DIPLO, BOYS NOIZE, SBTRKT, SIMIAN MOBILE DISCO, CHASE & STATUS
>
> **TICKET PRICE:** ✪✪✪
>
> **ACCOMMODATION:** ✪✪✪
>
> **PRICE OF BEER:** ✪✪✪✪
>
> **PRICE OF CIGARETTES:** ✪✪✪✪
>
> **AVERAGE COST OF A SNACK AT THE FESTIVAL:** ✪✪✪

# Creamfields

## CHESHIRE, ENGLAND

The name paints quite a beautiful picture — fields full of fluffy white cream, lovely. In reality though, Creamfields is a no-nonsense weekend of solid raving strictly for the headstrong (in other words, Scousers). It's a dance music festival that was launched by the company behind one of Britain's greatest former clubbing institutions — Cream. In the nineties the club was THE place to be if you were raving up north, holding its own during the boom times, when superstar DJs like Tall Paul, Judge Jules, Paul Oakenfold, and Pete Tong were at their peak. The cash that flowed into the club allowed its owners to start up Creamfields, a weekend-long debauched affair based on the ideals of the club combined with a festival mentality. It made for a winning formula and has been running since 1998, the original location being Winchester.

Like the famous club that gave birth to it, Creamfields is a haven for ravers and pulls in the biggest names in dance music year after year. From Jamie Jones to Tiesto and every DJ in between, the line-ups at the festival are always impressive and endless. No wonder the UK original attracts over 30,000 visitors every year.

There are the typical problems you'll find at any British festival though, mainly based around the rain... and chavs – both easy to predict and protect yourself against though. Don't let them put you off, if there's one festival in the UK that truly embodies the spirit of the rave, its Creamfields.

If proof were ever needed of how successful the festival's formula is, it's the fact that it's been transported around the world,

DATE: AUGUST BANK HOLIDAY WEEKEND

PAST HEADLINERS: THE PRODIGY, SKREAM, BENGA, TIÉSTO, ARMAND VAN HELDEN, PAUL VAN DYK, RICHIE HAWTIN, DEADMAU5, DAVID GUETTA

TICKET PRICE: ✪✪✪✪

ACCOMMODATION: ✪✪✪

PRICE OF BEER: ✪✪✪✪

PRICE OF CIGARETTES: ✪✪✪✪

AVERAGE COST OF A SNACK AT THE FESTIVAL: ✪✪✪✪

with various international incarnations taking place in slightly more exotic locations than the north-west of England—Peru, Brazil, Abu Dhabi, and Buenos Aires among them. Fields of cream for everyone!

# Download

## DONNINGTON PARK, ENGLAND

If you like to shake your long hair rocker-style and take pride in your complete collection of Iron Maiden LPs, or your idea of a perfect Saturday night out is an evening throwing yourself around a mosh pit with 200 like-minded souls, then Download, the UK's premier rock festival, is the one place you need to be heading.

Download started as the bastard spawn of Monsters Of Rock, a legendary one-day festival that took place at Donnington Park during the eighties and nineties. Owned by concert giants Live Nation, it all started in 2003 as a continuation of Monsters Of Rock's musical policy, offering the finest guitar bands around to a new generation of festival-goers. Initially running over two days, it was extended to a three-day metal mash-up in 2005 in order to reward the hoardes of dedicated fans who come from all over Europe and further afield to bask in the glow of some of rock 'n' rolls brightest stars.

> DATE: MID-JUNE
> PAST HEADLINERS: IRON MAIDEN, SLIPKNOT, MOTÖRHEAD, GUNS 'N' ROSES, BLACK SABBATH, HIM, ENTER SHIKARI, SYSTEM OF A DOWN
> TICKET PRICE: ✪✪✪
> ACCOMMODATION: ✪✪✪
> PRICE OF BEER: ✪✪✪✪
> PRICE OF CIGARETTES: ✪✪✪✪
> AVERAGE COST OF A SNACK AT THE FESTIVAL: ✪✪✪✪

Now in its 11th year, Download is a beer-fueled rockfest like no other in the UK. Legends like AC/DC, Iron Maiden, Marilyn Manson, Metallica, Iggy & The Stooges, and many more rock Gods have graced the main stage there, or rather torn the stage to shreds and danced on its sorry remains! Alongside the leather-and-denim clad deities you will also find some of the best new bands the scene has to offer spread across the six stages. With so much music to see, it's more than enough to keep any metal fan happy.

# Eastern Electrics

## KNEBWORTH PARK, ENGLAND

A relatively new face to appear on the UK festival circuit, Eastern Electrics is the festival incarnation of a well-respected London rave institution. EE is famed for its New Year's Eve parties and other such warehouse-based dalliances, mainly based in east London. In 2012 they announced their very first attempt at a festival, using their organizational expertise and superb industry contacts to amass a huge line-up and secure a decent spot in the Docklands area of south-east London.

It went well and, in 2013, Eastern Electrics morphed from a one-day event into a far bigger three-dayer, moving out of London to beautiful Knebworth Park, where Oasis, the Rolling Stones, and Robbie Williams famously held huge concerts. Poor Robbie fans were left disappointed as Knebworth was taken over by some of the finest names in electronic music—including Seth Troxler, Dixon, Maceo Plex, and Prosumer—rather than the warbling Angels crooner.

DATE: EARLY AUGUST

PAST HEADLINERS: MAYA JANE COLES, KERRI CHANDLER, DAVE CLARKE, BEN UFO, RICHIE HAWTIN, CLAUDE VON STROKE

TICKET PRICE: ✪✪✪

ACCOMMODATION: ✪✪

PRICE OF BEER: ✪✪✪

PRICE OF CIGARETTES: ✪✪✪

AVERAGE COST OF A SNACK AT THE FESTIVAL: ✪✪✪

# Farr Festival

## HERTFORDSHIRE, ENGLAND

A deserted forest, perfect for shenanigans and shaking a leg or two, whether it's day or night. Farr Festival takes this location and converts it into an underground rave for a few thousand party people. With a considered approach and a "boutique" feel to it (i.e. small and intimate), Farr is already widely-respected despite the fact it's only been around for a couple of years. This is mainly due to the strength of its line-ups, which have featured Julio Bashmore, Terry Farley, Waifs & Strays, and The Neon Lights among many others.

DATE: MID-JULY

PAST HEADLINERS: BICEP, EATS EVERYTHING, SUBB-AN, ANDY WEATHERALL, DBRIDGE

TICKET PRICE: ✪✪✪

ACCOMMODATION: ✪✪

PRICE OF BEER: ✪✪✪✪

PRICE OF CIGARETTES: ✪✪✪✪

AVERAGE COST OF A SNACK AT THE FESTIVAL: ✪✪✪✪

Because of the woodland location there's a naughty feel to Farr, as though you've run away to the Hertfordshire countryside with a few mates and nothing else apart from a few bottles of cider and enough cigarettes for the weekend. When combined with a great atmosphere and (fingers crossed!) even better weather, that mischievous feeling permeates throughout the duration of the festival, making Farr one of those must-do events that's likely to become a firm fixture on the annual raving calendar for many Brits and overseas visitors, too.

# We Are FSTVL

## DAMYN'S HALL AERODROME, ESSEX, ENGLAND

**2013** saw a new addition to the multitude of festivals that take place across the UK: We Are FSTVL. The name sounded a little self-important, but the festival boasted possibly one of the biggest electronic music line-ups the UK had ever seen, so perhaps it had a good reason to sound self-assured!

With a music policy aimed squarely at dance fans, We Are FSTVL takes place in Essex, undoubtedly the mecca of "deep house" in Britain at the moment (how did that happen; answers on a postcard please!). Anyway, regardless of the fake tan quota, the first installment measured a 9.0 on the raving Richter scale—Ricardo Villalobos played an incredible three-hour set; techno king Sven Vath killed it, as did Eats Everything, DJ Sneak, Mistajam, P Money... the list is endless. The only complaint ravers had was that they couldn't clone themselves in order to see everyone they wanted! The setting was also a hit with the punters, ensuring all who attended had an unforgettable experience. We can't wait for next year...

DATE: LAST WEEKEND IN MAY

PAST HEADLINERS: SVEN VATH, RPR SOUNDSYSTEM, GUY GERBER, RUDIMENTAL, DIXON, SUBFOCUS, KERRI CHANDLER, BODDIKA, DAMIAN LAZERUS, MR C

TICKET PRICE: ✪✪

ACCOMMODATION: ✪✪✪✪

PRICE OF BEER: ✪✪✪✪

PRICE OF CIGARETTES: ✪✪✪✪

AVERAGE COST OF A SNACK AT THE FESTIVAL: ✪✪✪✪

# Field Day

## VICTORIA PARK, EAST LONDON, ENGLAND

If you live in London and are too lazy to leave the capital then east London's Victoria Park is where you can find the Field Day Festival (along with Lovebox later in the season). Not that it's purely for lazy festival goers, far from it. Field Day is considered by some to be one of the biggest mash-ups of the year, with plenty of people traveling into London to join the locals and get stuck into the frivolities.

This makes for an interesting mixture of people, some of whom can stagger home once the stage lights are turned down whilst others who turn up with nowhere to stay end up diving right into the deep end; overindulging at one of the many afterparties.

The setting is Victoria Park, a rather picturesque area of greenery where joggers and bike riders keep fit side-by-side. It's a serene place perfect for a romantic walk or picnic, but when Field Day is on this place is turned on its head. The Village Mentality area has lots of fun and games—imagine a village fete where everyone is either drunk, high, or both and you're on the right track. The festival didnt get its name by accident, anyone who loves a raucous time or likes to let loose is literally going to have a field day.

> **DATE:** LAST WEEKEND IN MAY
> **PAST HEADLINERS:** JUSTICE, THE HORRORS, JAMES BLAKE, MODESELEKTOR, FOALS, FOUR TET, SBTRKT, DJANGO DJANGO, BAT FOR LASHES
> **TICKET PRICE:** ✪✪✪
> **ACCOMMODATION:** ✪✪✪✪
> **PRICE OF BEER:** ✪✪✪✪
> **PRICE OF CIGARETTES:** ✪✪✪✪
> **AVERAGE COST OF A SNACK AT THE FESTIVAL:** ✪✪✪✪

The festival started in 2007 and hasn't looked back since, with a vast array of artists appearing on its eclectic line-ups over the years. From Caribou and Mumford & Sons through to Mystery Jets, Matthew Dear, and Fake Blood, Field Day is always up to speed with the performers it hires, who act as the catalyst for plenty of good times. So, if you want to get wrecked in Victoria Park and not have the police called on you, try Field Day.

# Glade

## HOUGHTON HALL, KING'S LYNN, ENGLAND

A festival that has had plenty of ups and downs since its inception back in 2003... Glade is built on character and is fortunate to have survived as long as it has. For those reasons, it has a strong and loyal following, priding itself on an alternative take on the festival mold, offering ticket holders a solid line-up and plenty to see and do, year after year.

---

**DATE:** VARIES

**PAST HEADLINERS:** CARL CRAIG, UNDERWORLD, ANDY C, RUSKO, VITALIC, FUNCTION, PENDULUM, TRENTEMØLLER, SVEN VATH, TRICKY, DJ MARKY, DJ FRESH, BOOKA SHADE, TODDLA T, BODIKA, ADDISON GROOVE, DILLINJA, PREQ NASTY, DUB PISTOLS, LEVON VINCENT, PROSUMER, BLAWAN

**TICKET PRICE:** ✪✪✪

**ACCOMMODATION:** ✪✪✪

**PRICE OF BEER:** ✪✪✪✪

**PRICE OF CIGARETTES:** ✪✪✪✪

**AVERAGE COST OF A SNACK AT THE FESTIVAL:** ✪✪✪✪

---

Glade originally started as an arena at Glastonbury festival (see page 24) and quickly grew in popularity, leading the owners to break away and start their own festival with a large degree of success. In 2007, the very first edition attracted over 16,000 people—not bad going, hey? In the following years, things really began to take shape. As well as its infallible music policy—UNKLE, Jeff Mills, Richie Hawtin, Andy C, Krafty Kuts, and Derrick May are just a few names from the world of dance music who have graced the stages at Glade—the festival also evolved to include interactive art installations, cabaret performances, and plenty of "back to earth" areas, where ravers could be "healed" from their ills and simply chill out.

Issues with the location hampered the festival a few years ago. In 2007, severe flooding threatened to bring Glade to a close but, fortunately, everyone soldiered on and, with the aid of a few rubber dinghies and free water wings for all ticket holders (probably), the festival lived to see another day. Then in 2010 Glade's owners had to cancel the festival: due to the growing numbers of attendees, the local

constabulary, annoyingly, decided to raise policing costs from £29,000 in 2009 to £175,000. Nice! In 2011, Glade returned and reduced the size of the festival to only 5,500 guests and moved to a new location, Houghton Hall in Norfolk, having already moved from the Wasing Estate in Berkshire to Matterley Bowl in Winchester.

The 2012 edition was, by all accounts, an absolute cracker, but sadly organizers decided to take 2013 off in order to regroup and reassess the festival. However, there is some good news as the promoters promise to be back in 2014 with what they describe as "the Glade festival of all festivals."

So as you can gather, Glade has been through quite a lot, but that's what gives the festival its character. The determination of the owners and the faithful followers has given it strength and made it a worthwhile destination... if you can actually work out where it's actually being held, that is!

# Glastonbury

## WORTHY FARM, SOMERSET, ENGLAND

Glastonbury is possibly the best-known festival in the world and certainly the biggest Europe has to offer, with an average of 150,000 attendees over the course of five days. It is also one of the longest running festivals of its kind, having been conceived in 1970, and has attracted some of the biggest artists in the history of popular music.

The very first festival to be held at Worthy Farm was called the Pilton Pop, Rock & Blues Festival, arranged by local farmer Michael Eavis. It was attended by around 1,500 people who each bought a ticket for £1 (US $1.50)—a far cry from the £205 (US $325) price tag on 2013's tickets. That £1 ticket gave you the chance to watch headliners T.Rex and also included free milk for every attendee. The festival took place sporadically throughout the seventies, with infrequent gatherings and festivals celebrating Stonehenge and the Summer Solstice. In 1981 Michael Eavis decided to take more control and turn the festival into an annual event.

DATE: END OF JUNE

PAST HEADLINERS: ARCTIC MONKEYS, RADIOHEAD, U2, JAY-Z, THE WHITE STRIPES, PAUL MCCARTNEY, OASIS, COLDPLAY, THE WHO, BLUR, KINGS OF LEON, STEVIE WONDER, ROLLING STONES, MUMFORD & SONS, DAVID BOWIE

TICKET PRICE: ⬤⬤⬤⬤⬤

ACCOMMODATION: ⬤⬤⬤⬤

PRICE OF BEER: ⬤⬤⬤⬤

PRICE OF CIGARETTES: ⬤⬤⬤⬤

AVERAGE COST OF A SNACK AT THE FESTIVAL: ⬤⬤⬤⬤

In the years since, Glasto has grown into a beast of a festival, with thousands of superstar performers playing on its hallowed soil—from Oasis and the Rolling Stones to Paul McCartney, Muse, Beyonce, Jay-Z, Coldplay, and countless other lesser-known acts. In fact, one of Glastonbury's most impressive features is its almost endless list of stages and areas available to explore. In recent years the festival has consisted of over 700 performers and 80 stages set across around 900 acres of land. Insane. This also means that it's possible to find pretty much every kind of music you can imagine. For as much as it's a festival that attracts huge headliners, there are also plenty of fringe

artists and those who occupy the more "underground" end of the musical spectrum. House, techno, dubstep, folk, indie, punk, hip hop, reggae, jazz, funk, latin, ska, pop—you name it, Glastonbury has it. In fact, even if you've never heard of it before, Glasto almost certainly has it, too!

If the variety of music isn't enough to keep you entertained, elsewhere on the festival site you can find a whole variety of weird and wonderful people and places to keep you busy. Take the Theatre and Circus field, for example, which offers performances ranging from jugglers and acrobats to cabaret artists and poets. Or there's the Pilton Palais cinema tent showing amazing music documentaries alongside recent blockbusters. If you want to get into a political debate there are plenty of organizations you can visit to work out how to change the world. If altruism is your thing, Glastonbury has had a long association with numerous good causes, particularly Oxfam, WaterAid, and Greenpeace, helping to transform the lives of disadvantaged people around the world.

One of the most influential aspects of Glastonbury's history is that it's a festival based on hippie ideals: the festival began life at a time when the world was occupied with peace and love. For that reason, there is a still a very "back-to-earth" atmosphere at Glastonbury and, although its clientele is as varied as one can imagine, the festival fundamentally remains very true to its hippie roots. In the Healing Field you can find all manner of masseurs, mystics, psychics, and healers. The fact that the festival site itself is located on some very important ley lines also adds to the free-spirited nature of Glasto and encourages people to lower their inhibitions, making for quite a spectacle.

Fancy dress is almost obligatory now, and don't be surprised if you see some very strange behavior at times, particularly around the stone circle at sunrise or the Shangri-La area, which really gets going once the main stages have finished, catering for those who want to carry on partying well into the next day. By 5am on the Monday morning this part of the festival is a very scary place indeed!

Glastonbury is a world away from the humdrum of everyday life—it's a temporary town where the world is turned on its head for a few days. As the blueprint for many festivals in both the UK and overseas, Glasto remains a firm favorite with ravers around the world.

For a festival virgin this is the equivalent of diving into the deep end without your water wings for the first time. But as one of the original UK festivals it's a must-see, and something every festival lover has to do at least once in their life.

# Global Gathering

## LONG MARSTON, WARWICKSHIRE, ENGLAND

You could say that the Birmingham-based Global Gathering is the arch enemy of Creamfields (see page 14). Launched by another former UK clubbing institution, Gods Kitchen (if, like me, you're old enough to remember Gods Kitchen then you may be a little too old to be reading this book!), it's basically a very similar set-up to the Liverpool festival but in a different part of the UK. So what it lacks in Scousers, it more than makes up for in Brummies!

Global is a bit younger than Creamfields, having started in 2001, but almost everything else about it—from the music policy to the crowd it attracts—is very similar. The first ever Global Gathering amassed a ridiculous line-up, featuring everyone from Steve Lawler through to Roni Size, MJ Cole, Lisa Lashes and plenty more, and brought more than 25,000 people to Long Marston Airfield for the festivities. Since then it has gone from strength to strength. The 2013 edition saw underground DJs like 2ManyDJs, Ferry Corsten, High Contrast, and Carl Cox all take to the decks alongside more pop-orientated artists like Example, Plan B, and Rita Ora.

GG has twice been voted the UK's Best Festival in DJ Mag's annual awards, and the brand has been replicated around the globe enjoying successful stints in Miami, Turkey, Poland, Belarus, and Malaysia to name but a few. Makes you wonder how well the Birmingham accent goes down in those locations...

DATE: END OF JULY

PAST HEADLINERS: SASHA, CARL COX, DAVID GUETTA, SKRILLEX, ARMIN VAN BUUREN, STEVE ANGELLO

TICKET PRICE: ✪✪✪

ACCOMMODATION: ✪✪✪

PRICE OF BEER: ✪✪✪✪

PRICE OF CIGARETTES: ✪✪✪✪

AVERAGE COST OF A SNACK AT THE FESTIVAL: ✪✪✪✪

# Isle of Wight Festival

## ISLE OF WIGHT, HAMPSHIRE, ENGLAND

Although the Isle of Wight is a small island off the south coast of the UK with, apparently, not a lot going on (aside from two prisons), it does play host to more than its fair share of musical events. There's Bestival (see page 10), but there's also the cleverly titled Isle of Wight Festival, where pop, rock, and several other genres combine to create a lovely few days of partying in the true festival spirit.

A few years back I caught some legendary acts there: The Sex Pistols, Iggy & The Stooges, The Police, Ian Brown, The Sugababes. No really, I did.

The Isle of Wight Festival is great because there's no pretence; you'll meet parents partying with their kids, couples, "up-for-it" youngsters, and more. It may not have the hedonistic atmosphere that fellow islander Bestival has, but not everyone wants to rave in a tree with midgets. Some people want to listen to good music with friends in a pleasant setting, and that's fine. That's not to play down IOW Festival, it's a hell of a lot of fun, too. And the Creole food stall is heaven on earth. I can still taste it now, mmmmm.

DATE: MID-JUNE

PAST HEADLINERS: PEARL JAM, BON JOVI, STONE ROSES, KINGS OF LEON, BLONDIE

TICKET PRICE: ✪✪✪

ACCOMMODATION: ✪✪✪

PRICE OF BEER: ✪✪✪✪

PRICE OF CIGARETTES: ✪✪✪✪

AVERAGE COST OF A SNACK AT THE FESTIVAL: ✪✪✪✪

# Latitude

## HENHAM PARK, SUFFOLK, ENGLAND

Held in Henham Park, Suffolk, Latitude is one of those festivals that caters for the more discerning raver. In amongst all the bands and other musical entertainment, there's literature, poetry, acting, and cabaret. That doesn't mean it's a pompous event, full of snooty people reading the latest literary papers aloud for all to hear, but instead it offers plenty of alternatives to the standard band-on-stage format you get at most festivals, which makes for a welcome change.

Music-wise, there's loads going on and over the years Snow Patrol, Damien Rice, Patrick Wolf, Bat For Lashes, and Paolo Nutini have all played there. The comedy line-up is also just as strong: Alan Carr and Eddie Izzard are notable performers, as are the world's best musical comedy act, The Horrors. Then there are the literary, theater, and spoken word stages to check out. It's this clever combination of all forms of entertainment that make Latitude one of the UK's best kept festival secrets and most definitely worth a visit!

DATE: MID-JULY

PAST HEADLINERS: KRAFTWERK, BLOC PARTY, BON IVER, ELBOW, VAMPIRE WEEKEND

TICKET PRICE: ✪✪✪✪

ACCOMMODATION: ✪✪✪

PRICE OF BEER: ✪✪✪

PRICE OF CIGARETTES: ✪✪✪

AVERAGE COST OF A SNACK AT THE FESTIVAL: ✪✪✪

# Leeds & Reading

## BRAMHAM PARK, LEEDS AND RICHFIELD AVENUE, READING, ENGLAND

Known for being more focused on rock and indie music than other genres, Reading and Leeds festivals are hugely popular — with the former running in one form or another since the seventies. A colorful history, including a council ban in the mid-eighties, has made Reading an institution on the UK festival landscape, and in 1999 the festival expanded to add a second leg, Leeds, to the fray.

Both are beer-soaked weekends of pure madness and headbanging—like V Festival's (see page 42) wizened old uncle who still goes out and parties just as hard as the youngsters. Ever since they both came into being, Leeds and Reading have managed to pull in the big guns, including Kurt Cobain in a wheelchair. Yes, in 1992, the late, great Nirvana frontman took to the stage, in

what was to be his last ever UK performance, pushed along in a wheelchair in an attempt to spoof newspaper reports about his health. Other noteworthy incidents include rapper 50 Cent being bottled by fans during his short-lived appearance back in 2004. In fact the hail of bottles was enough to send the rap star (who was once shot nine times during a gun attack in New York) running for cover—after throwing his mic into the crowd, of course. Not quite the Candy Shop he was expecting.

So, if you fancy breaking the world record for the quickest "bottle* off stage", or you're just keen to get boozed up and have a bounce to some quality music, Reading and Leeds are where it's at.

* This book in no way encourages bottling!

**DATE:** END OF AUGUST

**PAST HEADLINERS:** GREEN DAY, EMINEM, RADIOHEAD, ARCTIC MONKEYS, THE PRODIGY, ARCADE FIRE, WEEZER, BLINK-182, QUEENS OF THE STONE AGE, NOFX, DEFTONES, MY CHEMICAL ROMANCE, MUSE, FLORENCE AND THE MACHINE, THE STROKES

**TICKET PRICE:** ✪✪✪

**ACCOMMODATION:** ✪✪✪✪

**PRICE OF BEER:** ✪✪✪

**PRICE OF CIGARETTES:** ✪✪✪✪

**AVERAGE COST OF A SNACK AT THE FESTIVAL:** ✪✪✪

# Lovebox

## VICTORIA PARK, LONDON, ENGLAND

Like Field Day (see page 20), Lovebox is held at Victoria Park, although its premise is slightly different being as it is a predominantly electronic music-based festival — that is, house, techno, drum 'n' bass. However, it has widened its appeal in recent years by bringing in some good old indie to attract a broader cross-section of festival-goers. So expect to see a fair few long-haired, pasty-skinned boppers in amongst the trendy deep-house heads.

DATE: MID-JULY

PAST HEADLINERS: GROOVE ARMADA, N.E.R.D., HOT CHIP, LANA DEL REY, GOLDFRAPP, BLONDIE, JAMIE JONES, DJ HARVEY, AZEALIA BANKS, FLYING LOTUS, MAGNETIC MAN, CRYSTAL CASTLES, SUB FOCUS, THE RAPTURE, BOBBY WOMACK, EMELI SANDÉ, SKREAM, PATRICK WOLF, SCISSOR SISTERS, MARC ALMOND, ROXY MUSIC, HERCULES & LOVE AFFAIR, ELLIE GOULDING, EMPIRE OF THE SUN

TICKET PRICE: ✪✪✪

ACCOMMODATION: ✪✪✪✪

PRICE OF BEER: ✪✪✪✪

PRICE OF CIGARETTES: ✪✪✪✪

AVERAGE COST OF A SNACK AT THE FESTIVAL: ✪✪✪✪

Having celebrated its 10th birthday in 2012, Lovebox is the brainchild of UK dance music legends Groove Armada, who initially launched it as a club night at the East London club 93 Feet East in 2002. To celebrate Lovebox surviving one year in London's often harsh clubbing scene, they decided to hold a one-day festival. They allocated 10,000 tickets for the party, which sold out in two days and, obviously realizing they were on to a good thing, the Groove Armada boys kept the festival side of Lovebox going.

Now held across three days, it's one of London's premier dance music events, attracting stellar line-ups and plenty of London's coolest electronic music enthusiasts, plus a fair few hangers-on looking to let their hair down for the weekend. There is no fancy dress here (unless you count the perma-tanned Essex mob in their bum bags and hi-top Nikes), but what you will find is the very best in hip hop, house, techno, and more. Over the years, various luminaries from the world of

music have appeared including Grace Jones, Snoop Dogg (or Snoop Lion as he now calls himself), Sly & the Family Stone, Jurassic 5, and, er, Duran Duran (who I love, by the way).

Best of all, unlike some of London's festivals, the sound levels in Victoria Park are actually pretty decent, which means you won't strain your ears trying to hear Maceo Plex's hot selection, or Ben Klock's relentless aural attack. Like most British festivals, though, make sure you keep an umbrella handy.

# Parklife

## MANCHESTER, ENGLAND

Manchester's newly-established, weekend-long festival has gone from strength to strength in recent years. Owned by the teams behind some of the city's most seminal events, including the Warehouse Project and Mad Ferret (a predecessor to Parklife), the festival encompasses everything that's great about Manchester's club scene, but it all takes place outdoors in south-central Manchester... Platt Fields to be precise. The stereotype of Manchester's population being "up for it," for the most part, pretty true, which means one hell of a party is in store for you if you're an out-of-towner. Parklife comes across as the northern equivalent of Lovebox (see page 32): a load of tents dotted around a park, all packed with top quality electronic music and, as the locals say, a "mad-fer-it" crowd bopping away all day and night.

Due to Parklife's central location, it's a really convenient festival to attend, with many of the same characteristics of country events, particularly the mud when it rains, but none of the stress of having to trek out to some country manor or a field in the middle of nowhere. So it's Goodbye Lord Farquar and his field of dreams, hello swaggering Liam Gallagher-esque park owner and his merry bunch of Madchester ravers. It's no walk in the park—more of a proper Mancunian swagger, and the city is much better off for it!

Since its inception in 2010, De La Soul, Horse Meat Disco, Chic (featuring Nile Rodgers), Flaming Lips, Dizzee Rascal, Goldie, and more have appeared on the line-up, bringing in a decent crowd and representing a whole host of genres. Make sure you're prepared for an intense weekend of partying both at the festival and the related after-parties that take place around the city during the Parklife weekend... a few months preparation at the gym should set you in good stead!

**DATE:** EARLY JUNE

**PAST HEADLINERS:** MARK RONSON, A-TRAK, JOHNNY MARR, EVERYTHING EVERYTHING, DJ SHADOW, AZEALIA BANKS,

**TICKET PRICE:** ✪✪✪

**ACCOMMODATION:** ✪✪✪

**PRICE OF BEER:** ✪✪✪✪

**PRICE OF CIGARETTES:** ✪✪✪✪

**AVERAGE COST OF A SNACK AT THE FESTIVAL:** ✪✪✪✪

# Rockness

## LOCH NESS, SCOTLAND

God gave rock and roll to you, as the famous song says, and the Scottish (with a little help from Fatboy Slim) gave Rockness to the rest of the world. As its clever name suggests, the festival takes place at the infamous Loch Ness, a site for monster-spotters from all over the world. Now, it's never been made clear, but there is an underlying suspicion that the organizers live in hope that the music from the festival might wake "Nessie" and bring her (or him) back to the surface for another breath of fresh air.

Do not be misled by the festival's name, although there is rock music on offer, Rockness also offers up plenty of dance music. It originally started when Fatty McFatboy took his Brighton Beach Party up to Scotland back in 2006. As with most modern-day festivals, it grew in size as demand for tickets increased every year and it now attracts

tonnes of headliners across eight large tents, with acts from techno legend Green Velvet through to Tinie Tempah, Kasabian, and The Prodigy. It must be said, the setting (Nessie or no Nessie) is beautiful and certainly makes a change from the muddy field locations used for most UK festivals. Of course, being based up in Scotland, the local influences are very strong—Scottish label Soma Records hosts a tent, as does Glasgow's well-known Sub Club— and you can't beat a good old Highland fling with the Scottish. Whatever the weather, they'll be swigging the booze, pogoing like there's no tomorrow, and making you feel right at home, no matter where you're from.

Make sure you take a camera with a telephoto lens with you, because you can never be sure when Nessie might rear her ugly head. You might end up being the one who caught the million dollar snap! That's if Fatboy Slim doesn't manage to get there first...

DATE: FIRST WEEK OF JUNE

PAST HEADLINERS: DAFT PUNK, DEADMAU5, MUMFORD & SONS, BIFFY CLYRO, DOVES, PENDULUM, IAN BROWN, THE PRODIGY

TICKET PRICE: ✪✪✪✪

ACCOMMODATION: ✪✪✪

PRICE OF BEER: ✪✪✪✪

PRICE OF CIGARETTES: ✪✪✪✪

AVERAGE COST OF A SNACK AT THE FESTIVAL: ✪✪✪✪

# Secret Garden Party

## ABBOTS RIPTON, CAMBRIDGESHIRE, ENGLAND

Taking place in Abbots Ripton, deep in the Cambridgeshire countryside, SGP (as it's fondly known) is a very special festival that has become a cult favorite thanks to the huge efforts of its creative team. A hub for the more bohemian and open-minded raver, SGP has quickly established itself as one of the go-to summer festivals in the UK, thanks to the rather colorful characters it attracts, its constant stream of fun and games, and the fact that many artists who play there consider it a "holiday," switching off completely to embrace the hedonism and often spending time mingling with members of the public.

**DATE:** FIRST WEEK OF JUNE

**PAST HEADLINERS:** REGINA SPEKTOR, DJANGO DJANGO, THE XX, JARVIS COCKER, THE NOISETTES, LYKKE LI, FLORENCE AND THE MACHINE

**TICKET PRICE:** ✪✪✪✪

**ACCOMMODATION:** ✪✪✪✪

**PRICE OF BEER:** ✪✪✪✪

**PRICE OF CIGARETTES:** ✪✪✪✪

**AVERAGE COST OF A SNACK AT THE FESTIVAL:** ✪✪✪✪

Started by Fred Fellowes back in 2004, Secret Garden Party was originally meant to be an alternative to the mainstream, more traditional festival. However, in the nine years since it was initiated, the party has grown in stature and is now, like it or not, very much a part of the mainstream UK festival landscape.

In terms of figures, the first Secret Garden Party attracted 1,000 people, while 2011's festival was attended by 26,000! Quite an impressive exponential growth, but one which amazingly has not affected the overall quality of proceedings. In fact, the swell in numbers means there are far more oddballs and eccentrics to increase the fun factor, as well as increasing the chances of losing your own marbles for a few days. Never seen a 7-foot tall Danish man flouncing around in a bespoke golden jacket covered in sequins? You will at SGP.

Aside from an eclectic selection of headliners, ranging from Goldie to Leftfield, Blondie, Gorillaz, and Orbital, one of the key aspects of SGP's popularity is its amazing attention to detail and jaw-dropping production. This is not just a collection of stages in a beautiful location, but an interactive, immersive experience that encourages everyone to participate in the fun and games on offer. Alongside the games that have included Drum 'n' Bass Boxing and Rebel Bingo, visitors can volunteer to take part in workshops, jump on art boats to take you on bewildering adventures, enjoy immersive installations, and you can even join in with helping to set up and take down everything at the festival.

2012's Secret Garden Party was probably one of the best so far, punctuated by an incredible fireworks display, skydivers, and an awesome airplane which drew a heart in the sky above the festival site—an epic event which many described as one of the best moments of their life.

# T In The Park

## BALADOO AIRFIELD, KINROSS, SCOTLAND

Scotland's premier festival has about everything one could wish for from a party: great music, a crazy crowd, fun, laughter, plenty of booze, and other such relaxants for the mind. Sometimes the sun even makes a rare appearance up there in the Highlands! T in the Park got its name from its sponsor, Tennents, allegedly the preferred beer of down-and-outs so, as you might expect, it's a wild affair from beginning to end. And if there's anyone who knows how to party, whatever the weather, it's the Scottish.

T in the Park started way back in 1994, when Rage Against the Machine, Primal Scream, Oasis, Blur, and the Manic Street Preachers were among the acts on the bill. In the 18 years that have passed, T in the Park has maintained its high caliber of artists and, as far as festivals are concerned, still remains Scotland's pride and joy. The music policy, encompassing a broad range of styles across seven stages, continues to be spot on and provides more than enough entertainment to keep the Scots, and those brave enough to venture that far north, in search of a good time, very happy. And with Tennents on tap throughout the day and night, you better be prepared to return home with the hangover to end all hangovers.

---

DATE: MID-JULY

PAST HEADLINERS: RIHANNA, THE KILLERS, MUSE, CALVIN HARRIS, SWEDISH HOUSE MAFIA, MADNESS, FOO FIGHTERS, PHOENIX, JAY-Z, KASABIAN

TICKET PRICE: ✪✪✪✪

ACCOMMODATION: ✪✪✪

PRICE OF BEER: ✪✪✪✪

PRICE OF CIGARETTES: ✪✪✪✪

AVERAGE COST OF A SNACK AT THE FESTIVAL: ✪✪✪✪

DATE: MID-AUGUST

PAST HEADLINERS: MERCURY REV, WILCO, SPIRITUALIZED, MARTHA WAINWRIGHT

TICKET PRICE: ✪✪✪

ACCOMMODATION: ✪✪✪

PRICE OF BEER: ✪✪✪✪

PRICE OF CIGARETTES: ✪✪✪✪

AVERAGE COST OF A SNACK AT THE FESTIVAL: ✪✪✪✪

# Wilderness

## CORNBURY PARK, OXFORDSHIRE, ENGLAND

You know what to expect from Wilderness when you find out that it's put on by the team behind Secret Garden Party (see page 38). Like a quiet little brother, Wilderness has been around for a while, but is relatively unassuming in comparison to its rambunctious older sibling. In fact, some compare it to "Secret Garden a few years ago — before the general public discovered it," whilst others have called it "Secret Garden Party for grown-ups." I think that statement is doing it a disservice; Wilderness is most definitely less glitzy in terms of its musical appeal but there's still a whole world of adventures to embark upon. Naked knitting? A bit dangerous if you ask me, but it's there on offer, right next to roller dancing, pop-up theatre shows, amazing food stalls, and all manner of adult delights, the likes of which your brain could probably never have even fathomed participating in.

Consider all the effort that goes into Secret Garden Party, but in a smaller space with less people, and making the decision to attend becomes a no-brainer, which is probably how you'll be described after a few mind-bending days out at Wilderness.

# V Festival

## HYLANDS PARK, ESSEX AND WESTON PARK, STAFFORDSHIRE, ENGLAND

Although V got its name from its sponsor — Virgin — the festival is not the brainchild of billionaire Richard Branson, as you might have thought. In fact, it was actually conceived by the rebellious and forward-thinking frontman from Pulp, Jarvis Cocker. Back in 1996 — at the height of his fame following his infamous bum-flashing protest during Michael Jackson's performance of Earth Song at the BRIT Awards — Jarvis declared that he wanted to perform two gigs in two days in two different towns. The idea was to entertain fans in both the north and the south of England over the course of a weekend, and it soon evolved into a music festival with other bands signed up to play both gigs. The festival still adheres to its original ideology with nearly all the acts performing at both events during the two days.

DATE: MID-JULY

PAST HEADLINERS: STONE ROSES, DAVID GUETTA, EMINEM, KASABIAN, BEADY EYE, BEYONCÉ, OASIS, SNOW PATROL, KAISER CHIEFS, AMY WINEHOUSE, RED HOT CHILI PEPPERS, FOO FIGHTERS, COLDPLAY, TOM JONES, THE SCRIPT

TICKET PRICE: ✪✪✪✪

ACCOMMODATION: ✪✪✪✪

PRICE OF BEER: ✪✪✪✪

PRICE OF CIGARETTES: ✪✪✪✪

AVERAGE COST OF A SNACK AT THE FESTIVAL: ✪✪✪✪

In the north of England, V was originally a Leeds-based event at Temple Newsam, before organizers of Leeds Festival (see page 30) swooped in and took over the site for themselves. It's now a firm fixture at Weston Park, Staffordshire. Meanwhile, in the south of the country, it has always been set in Hylands Park, Chelmsford.

V's foundations are based in rock music, and it remained true to this ethos for many years up until recently, when the music policy became a little more relaxed and pop acts were included on the line-ups. To some, V has become a festival for the casual festival-goer; that is, the type of person who likes their festival experience to be an easy-going one, with all their favorite chart acts on the bill. That's not to say it's a bad thing—pretty much every successful

festival needs a USP and should be attractive to a large clientele. Mass appeal is certainly what V is aiming for, and unashamedly so. Recent headliners have included Beyonce, Nicki Minaj, Rihanna, Emeli Sandé, and Calvin Harris alongside more traditional indie and rock bands like Kings of Leon and The Killers.

V is also a hotspot for many a British "celebrity," with its "VIP" area becoming a playground for all the many stars who appear on stage there, as well as a whole host of famous UK faces. From high-flying actors like Danny Dyer to Coleen Rooney, *Harry Potter* star Rupert Grint, and heroic cast members from reality show *The Only Way Is Essex*, there's a never-ending list of showbiz darlings to rub shoulders with in the VIP area.

# Chapter 2

## Europe

# 10 Days Off

## GHENT, BELGIUM

Though Belgium has an unfounded reputation for being boring, it actually plays host to a fair few festivals — many of them highly regarded by the discerning raver out there (of which there are plenty, I can assure you). The festival originally started out in 1995 as "10 Days of Techno," but obviously somewhere along the line a wise person decided that 10 days of techno was a bit much, so maybe they should consider playing some music other than techno, like tech house, maybe? Or ambient techno? Or house with a "techy" flavor? Tech-inspired garage could be an option. You know, anything that's a bit different from techno.

**DATE:** MID-JULY

**PAST HEADLINERS:** FELIX DA HOUSECAT, HOT CHIP, JESSE ROSE, NICOLAS JAAR, BENGA, TODD TERJE, MISS KITTEN, ROBERT HOOD, NACEO PLEX, MATTHEW DEAR, JACKMASTER, BICEP, MIDLAND, LINDSTROM, EGYPTIAN HIP HOP

**TICKET PRICE:** ✪

**ACCOMMODATION:** ✪✪

**PRICE OF BEER:** ✪✪

**PRICE OF CIGARETTES:** ✪✪

**AVERAGE COST OF A SNACK AT THE FESTIVAL:** N/A

Over the years, the line-ups have included acts from one extreme to another—in 1996, for instance, synth pop legend Jimmy Somerville was on the same bill as drum 'n' bass dons 4Hero. Since then, the policy has always covered many different dance music genres, from dubstep through to deep house, with artists from both the new school and old. 2013's edition saw appearances from Vondelpark, Space Dimension Controller, James Zabiela, Matthew Dear, Metro Area, Deadboy, Gui Boratto, and plenty more.

It's a festival with a formula that has kept it alive for 19 years and it still remains one of the best electronic music events in Belgium, which definitely is NOT as boring as people make it out to be. A great festival and a great advertisement for Belgium's party scene.

# ADE

## AMSTERDAM, HOLLAND

ADE, or Amsterdam Dance Event has a debatable status; is it a festival or more of a music conference? Either way, I decided to include it because a) once there, you can party non-stop for almost a week, and b) it's my aim to inform the reader through the power of word about any occasion where there's the option to go raving for 24 hours or more.

ADE is primarily an excuse for all the most important (and not so important) people in electronic music to get together, stand in the street outside the Felix Martis building in central Amsterdam, and carry out the same kind of conversations they usually have via email. Inside the Felix and the connecting Dylan Hotel, lots of conferences take place discussing the past, present, and future of electronic music. It's all quite professional and rather sensible.

DATE: MID-OCTOBER

PAST HEADLINERS: RICHIE HAWTIN, LOCO DICE, CARL COX, PAUL OAKENFOLD, DAVE CLARKE, JORIS VOORN, JOHN DIGWEED, CHRIS LIEBING, CARIBOU, AME, DUBFIRE, SETH TROXLER, PETE TONG, SOUL CLAP

TICKET PRICE: ✪✪

ACCOMMODATION: ✪✪ TO ✪✪✪✪

PRICE OF BEER: ✪✪✪

PRICE OF CIGARETTES: ✪✪✪

AVERAGE COST OF A SNACK AT THE FESTIVAL: ✪✪✪

However, outside of this, there are hundreds of parties spread out over 75 locations, with all the world's best DJs taking center stage to rock Amsterdam's clubs. This is where things gets interesting for anyone who's not an agent, booker, PR, journalist, or any other music industry professional! Over the course of five days, Amsterdam's clubs play host to everyone from Masters At Work and David Guetta to Maya Jane Coles and Maceo Plex. Everything from the hardest techno to the most commercial trance is catered for and the parties happen EVERY night. As I said, not strictly a festival, but still some of the best parties in the world and that's what this book is all about.

# Audioriver

## PLOCK, POLAND

Polish people can shake a leg or two, we all know that. Well, maybe we don't, but we will once we've been to Audioriver, a music and arts festival that focuses on... yes, you've guessed it, electronic music. Now, I know what you're probably thinking, "There are so many electronic music festivals out there, why should I choose one in Poland?" But don't let the fact that there are plenty of other, more traditional party destinations out there put you off. A festival's selling point is not just based on music and if you're buying a ticket just for the line-up, especially at an overseas event, then I suggest you just stay at home and find one closer to where you live. It'll most likely feature similar artists and you'll save yourself some money, too.

DATE: END OF JULY

PAST HEADLINERS: RÖYKSOPP, RADIO SLAVE, RUDIMENTAL, MR OIZO, STEFFI, GUSGUS

TICKET PRICE: ✪

ACCOMMODATION: ✪

PRICE OF BEER: ✪

PRICE OF CIGARETTES: ✪

AVERAGE COST OF A SNACK AT THE FESTIVAL: ✪

However, if you've got a slightly more open-minded approach to festival going, the best thing about attending an overseas event is experiencing another culture. New people, new food, new drinks; those are the things that make the foreign festival visit one to remember (or totally forget, or one to try really really hard to remember... and fail).

But I digress... Audioriver is a great festival, recently receiving a nomination for Best Medium-sized Festival at the Festival Awards Europe. It's attended by over 15,000 people (that's a lot of Polish ravers!) who come to see artists including Goldie, Kavinsky, Marco Carola, and Zombie Nation. The festival is held on a beach, which makes for some interesting dance moves, ever shuffled on sand without falling over? It's not easy! Something that the festival prides itself on is never booking the same act twice, which, I must say, is quite an achievement considering its five-year history.

# Balaton Sound

## LAKE BALATON, HUNGARY

If house, techno, and drum 'n' bass aren't your bag, by now you may well be a little tired of hearing about electronic music festivals. Balaton Sound is billed as an electronic music festival, BUT its policy is very loose and previous headliners have included The Beastie Boys, The Brand New Heavies, The B-52s, and lots more groups that begin with "The." It all started in 2007, beside one of the largest lakes in Europe — Lake Balaton. In just a few short years, the event has grown to attract over 100,000 punters, and winning Best Medium-sized Festival at the European Festival Awards. Ace!

What I like best about Balaton is that the organizers nurture their own scene by booking a large number of Hungarian acts, which is something that other parties around the world should really do more. A lot of festivals simply ignore local talent for the sake of bringing in large international acts. Of course, this brings in the numbers and the cash, but it's important to support your national treasures too and encourage new acts. Balaton does this very well and should be highly commended, maybe at an award ceremony for festivals or something.

---

**DATE:** SECOND THURSDAY IN JULY

**PAST HEADLINERS:** WU-TANG CLAN, MASSIVE ATTACK, NAS, MOBY, GOSSIP

**TICKET PRICE:** ✪✪✪

**ACCOMMODATION:** ✪✪

**PRICE OF BEER:** ✪✪

**PRICE OF CIGARETTES:** ✪✪

**AVERAGE COST OF A SNACK AT THE FESTIVAL:** ✪✪

---

# Benicassim

## BENICASSIM, SPAIN

Summer festivals in the north of Europe have many factors that can make camping a very uncomfortable experience; from torrential rain flooding your tent to ice-cold temperatures that will chill you to the core (or both!). On the other hand, at Benicassim the biggest problem you're likely to face is the extreme heat, which can be so uncomfortable it's not uncommon for people to sleep outside their tents. And that's probably the only complaint you'll hear from anyone who goes there — hardly a big issue compared with bad weather, is it? Due to the sun, Benicassim is just as popular with UK festival goers as it is with the local Spanish, which is all good and means the crowds are usually pretty mixed. The line-ups are pretty eclectic, too, and the stages at Benicassim offer up a wide variety of talent — from Oasis to Justice — to get stuck into.

Having mentioned the weather, it seems even a Mediterranean festival is still under threat from the elements. Benicassim made the headlines in 2009 when high winds battered the festival and a fire broke out dangerously close to a campsite. This combination of wind and fire (earth decided not to get involved) caused people to be evacuated from their tents and several bands, including the Kings of Leon, had to cancel their performances. Benicassim was in the news again in 2010 when Skream and Benga were banned from the festival for good after encouraging a stage invasion by their fans at the end of their set, and once again in 2012 when the company behind Benicassim went bust, putting its future in serious doubt. However, Vince Power, head of the events company that owns Benicassim, managed to salvage the event, which celebrated its ninth year in 2013. Happy, sweaty days for all!

DATE: MID-JULY

PAST HEADLINERS: BOB DYLAN, BEADY EYE, THE KILLERS, THE STROKES, THE PIXIES

TICKET PRICE: ✪✪✪

ACCOMMODATION: ✪✪

PRICE OF BEER: ✪✪

PRICE OF CIGARETTES: ✪✪

AVERAGE COST OF A SNACK AT THE FESTIVAL: ✪✪

# Berlin Festival

## BERLIN, GERMANY

Ah Berlin, home of the non-stop party and the perfect spot for a festival. Which brings me neatly to the cleverly titled, Berlin Festival — one of Europe's finest. Held at the disused Tempelhof Airport, this event is an essential destination for many a music lover. The music policy is second to none: The Pet Shop Boys, Blur, Justice, Ghostpoet, Little Dragon, and Franz Ferdinand have all taken to the stage, and that's just the tip of the proverbial iceberg. There are loads and loads more artists on Berlin Festival's awesome line-ups who, when combined with an amazing location makes it well worth a visit.

Then there's the Berliners themselves: cool, unassuming, and always ready to party... and party... and party some more. "What time is it? 2016 you say?! Oh great, so I've been partying for three years non-stop." This actually happens in Berlin, every day. If you don't believe me, simply go to the Berlin Festival for yourself and you'll soon see. Catch you in 2016, sucker!

DATE: EARLY SEPTEMBER

PAST HEADLINERS: BJÖRK, ELLIE GOULDING, MIA, PUBLIC ENEMY, DIPLO, SKRILLEX, SIGUR ROS, LCD SOUNDSYSTEM

TICKET PRICE: ✪✪✪

ACCOMMODATION: ✪✪✪

PRICE OF BEER: ✪✪✪

PRICE OF CIGARETTES: ✪✪✪

AVERAGE COST OF A SNACK AT THE FESTIVAL: ✪✪

# BOOM FESTIVAL

## IDANHA-A-NOVA, PORTUGAL

DATE: EVERY OTHER YEAR, OVER THE FULL MOON CLOSEST TO 1ST AUGUST

PAST HEADLINERS: GALA DROP, HATAKEN, AJJA, EMOK, -Z-

TICKET PRICE: ✪✪✪

ACCOMMODATION: ✪✪

PRICE OF BEER: ✪✪

PRICE OF CIGARETTES: ✪✪

AVERAGE COST OF A SNACK AT THE FESTIVAL: ✪✪

Boom is a festival in the traditional sense; a celebration of arts and culture, with a back-to-earth ideology and respecting nature and fellow humans. Everything about this festival is great and whether or not you're open to slightly more "hippified" ideals, there's a great atmosphere; it's in a great location and the music is pretty great. In fact, Boom was originally all about the music, before evolving into an arts and culture event. Nowadays, you can find people creating sculptures, doing yoga, painting, and performing street theater, as well as bubbling away to the latest drum 'n' bass, breakbeat, trance, techno, or whatever other kind of music you can think of.

There's also a very strong emphasis on multiculturalism and breaking down age stereotypes, so don't worry if you think you're a bit past it and someone bought you this book for a joke, there's room at Boom. Actually, there's room anywhere you want to go, no matter what your age, don't listen to anyone who says you're too old. I've seen parents at every festival I've been to, and as long as you're having a good time, who cares?!

But back to Boom... it's bright, colorful, full of wonderful characters, non-corporate, and has a very forward-thinking, open-minded ethos which makes it one of today's better festivals. Shame it only happens every two years though, booooooo(m)!

# Dimensions

## PULA, CROATIA

The baby brother of Outlook (see page 71), Dimensions operates in a slightly different area of the electronic music spectrum to it's older sibling. It goes for the house and techno jugular, bringing together eye-watering line-ups in the very same location as Outlook — Fort Punta Christo in Pula. Epic line-ups aside, it's an extraordinary location for a rave up, with some parties happening in the empty moats of the fort, whilst others take place on nearby beaches and, as with every Croatian festival, the boats that occupy the surrounding waters. Once inside the fort, you'll feel as though you've stepped back in time, with the the music and crowd offering the only indication that you are still in the 21st Century and not the 16th! If you do see any knights dancing shoulder to shoulder with the rest of the crowd, you might want to double check what you're smoking — the glorious weather makes it impossible for anyone to rock such an outfit... unless they're genuinely insane!

**DATE:** EARLY SEPTEMBER

**PAST HEADLINERS:** MR SCRUFF, GILLES PETERSON, BEN KLOCK, MOUNT KIMBIE, PANTHA DU PRINCE, THEO PARRISH, FLOATING POINTS, MALA IN CUBA, MARTYN, OMAR S, MOODYMANN

**TICKET PRICE:** ✪✪✪✪

**ACCOMMODATION:** ✪✪

**PRICE OF BEER:** ✪✪

**PRICE OF CIGARETTES:** ✪✪

**AVERAGE COST OF A SNACK AT THE FESTIVAL:** ✪✪

Having started in 2012, Dimensions is still in its infancy, but one thing's for certain—the festival is sure to continue to lay down the biggest and best music from the world of house and techno. 2013 saw Model 500 headline, accompanied by over 60 other artists including Ben UFO, Daphni, Levon Vincent, and Tony Allen. With line-ups this strong, Dimensions is set to grow and grow.

# Dour Festival

## DOUR, BELGIUM

To anyone who speaks English, dour means stern or harsh, which this festival could well be if you constantly overindulge during its four-day run. However, if you say the word Dour to a Belgian, he will instantly think of the town that has held a festival every year since 1989. Yes, 1989, remember that year? No? Shame. Anyway, Dour has been going for over 25 years and it's still running strong. In the beginning just five bands played but nowadays you can expect to encounter over 200 bands and DJs across six stages with an annual attendance of over 150,000. Immense.

Music at Dour is as diverse as you like, from reggae and electro to pop and dubstep (which are probably one and the same to some people), hardcore, death metal, and techno. For instance, at the 2013 installment, where Dour marked its 25th year, there were some very special appearances to help celebrate. It was an epic event that once again highlighted the festival's eclectic booking policy. Hardcore band Hatebreed shared the bill with soul singer Charles Bradley and electro DJ Erol Alkan, whilst "King of dancehall" Beenie Man, alt-rockers Smashing Pumpkins, and hip hop legends Wu-Tang Clan are just a few more examples of the hugely varied collection of artists that have appeared on stage at the festival. Are they good enough reasons to tempt you into buying a ticket? This is one those festivals that not many people will have heard of; I hope you will now investigate further and pay a visit.

DATE: MID-JULY

PAST HEADLINERS: YEAH YEAH YEAHS, THE VACCINES, TOOTS AND THE MAYTALS, SIMIAN MOBILE DISCO, FLYING LOTUS

TICKET PRICE: ✪✪✪

ACCOMMODATION: ✪

PRICE OF BEER: ✪✪

PRICE OF CIGARETTES: ✪✪

AVERAGE COST OF A SNACK AT THE FESTIVAL: ✪✪

# Exit

## NOVI SAD, SERBIA

Exit's history is, understandably, political — having sprung out of the oppressive regime set by Slobodan Milošević back in the late nineties. Three students were the brains behind the original festival that took place in 2000, set at the University of Novi Sad in the north of Serbia. It lasted 100 days and saw performances from many local Serbian musicians. Its slogan was "Exit out of ten years of madness," which was aimed directly at the political regime. Fast forward a few years and the location has changed, the political undertones remain, and the attendance numbers have exploded; as have the international line-up of performers.

DATE: MID-JULY

PAST HEADLINERS: GUNS N' ROSES, NEW ORDER, LCD SOUNDSYSTEM, PORTISHEAD, ARCADE FIRE, THE CHEMICAL BROTHERS, PATTI SMITH, KORN, N.E.R.D., BEASTIE BOYS, M.I.A., WU-TANG CLAN, PULP, FAITH NO MORE, BLOC PARTY

TICKET PRICE: ✪✪

ACCOMMODATION: ✪✪

PRICE OF BEER: ✪ TO ✪✪

PRICE OF CIGARETTES: ✪

AVERAGE COST OF A SNACK AT THE FESTIVAL: ✪✪

One of Exit's main selling points (of which there are many) is its amazing location: the Petrovordian Fortress located up on a hill overlooking the Danube River. It truly is a breathtaking and completely unique festival site, though it does get a little dusty! Exit also has an excellent record for decent weather, with the temperature being largely warm or hot. On top of this, the festival (which now lasts a slightly more manageable four days rather than the initial 100) can boast of one of the most diverse music policies of any festival anywhere in the world. Not content with securing main-stage headliners such as Jamiroquai, Korn, M.I.A, Placebo, and Editors, the festival also has a fully fledged Dance Arena—an incredible stage set up in a valley at the back of the fortress, spine-tinglingly good at sunrise—a rock stage, latin music, reggae, a stage for up-and-coming acts, plenty of local talent, and lots more. Altogether there are around 20 stages, all offering a different genre of music—there's even a Silent Disco.

Exit is also one of the cheapest festivals in the world, a four-day trip there still comes in at around US$475 (£300) for most visitors from western Europe, which is why a large percentage of revelers at the festival are Brits and backpackers in search of a bargain. A pint of beer is a steal at around US$1.50 (£1), as is a packet of cigarettes. The locals are about as friendly as you can imagine. Having been through the troubles of the past, they are often pleasantly surprised to find that people actually want to visit their country—so expect a warm welcome.

Novi Sad is a relatively small yet quaint town and, apart from the festival, has plenty to offer. The restaurants are all great—the local food is very good—and the "beach" is a sight to behold. The place I'm referring to is, in fact, a man-made sandy area located next to the Danube, just a few minutes walk out of the town center. This is a huge attraction, with music playing all day long and some of the most physically perfect specimens (male and female) you're ever likely to clap eyes on relaxing in the sun.

It's been around for over 13 years now and for very good reason; Exit is one of Europe's premier music festivals. Just make sure you're prepared to cough up several ounces of dust after partying there for four days straight!

# The Garden Festival

## TISNO, CROATIA

If you read this book from cover to cover, by the time you get to the end of the European chapter, you'll be tired of reading about festivals in Croatia, but it's a fact that some of Europe's very best outdoor music events take place on the Adriatic coast. A combination of a great summer climate, cheap food, cigarettes, and beer, and a seemingly endless list of amazing locations means that it's become a hub for European festivals.

Locationwise, Garden Festival in Tisno is one of the very best—the intimate, coastal setting makes for a sublime experience. Garden is small yet perfectly formed haven away from some of the crazier festivals that take place across Europe. Organizers have stayed strong and, rather than be greedy and open up the event to bigger and bigger crowds, have capped the event's capacity at 2,000, choosing to focus on quality and intimacy rather than financial gain. What some may refer to it as a "boutique" festival, it has grown a little since it was started but remains contained and true to its roots.

Garden also prides itself on curating diverse line-ups, mainly dance-music based, that never rely too heavily on the big-hitters. They tend to include many talented but perhaps lesser-known names alongside the headline acts. 2013's bill included Theo Parrish, Soul Clap, Wolf and

**DATE:** EARLY JULY

**PAST HEADLINERS:** TENSNAKE, NORMAN JAY, DIXON, ART DEPARTMENT, JACQUES RENAULT, BENOIT & SERGIO

**TICKET PRICE:** ✪✪✪✪

**ACCOMMODATION:** ✪✪✪

**PRICE OF BEER:** ✪✪

**PRICE OF CIGARETTES:** ✪✪

**AVERAGE COST OF A SNACK AT THE FESTIVAL:** ✪✪

Lamb, Psychemagik, Maurice Fulton, Bicep, Crazy P, Greg Wilson, Huxley, Tim Sweeney, Maxxi Soundsystem, Toby Tobias, Deep Space Orchestra, and PBR Streetgang to name but a few. Then there are the famous boat parties curated by some of UK's finest club nights and electronic music website Resident Advisor, plus nights hosted by New York's Beats in Space and record label Futureboogie.

A relaxed atmosphere is the key to Garden's success. Where other festivals are all about the adrenalin, there's an underlying feeling of serenity and a laid-back nature to most of those who pay the festival a visit. Some even use it as a "decompression holiday" after the madness of Hideout (see page 62).

# Hideout

## PAG, CROATIA

If ever there was an event that proved just how popular festivals in Europe have become, it's Hideout. In just three years it has developed into an essential destination for a large number of youngsters from the UK. Set along the coast at Zrce Beach on the Croatian island of Pag, it's already one of the most popular electronic music festivals in Europe — pretty crazy considering it's been around for such a short time. Croatia is often touted as the "new Ibiza," thanks to its beautiful weather, awe-inspiring locations, and countless festivals. To compare Croatia to the White Island is doing it a disservice as it's one of a kind and Hideout is just one of the jewels in its festival crown.

Zrce Beach is a hugely popular location within Croatia, although it's not exactly pure white sands, more like tiny stones that really don't benefit the barefoot beachgoer (NB: Always wear flip flops or sandals on Zrce Beach!). The main draw on the beach is its range of beachside clubs: Kalypso, Papaya, Aquarius... all of which operate day and night, with the latter two running their own pool parties to counteract the 30°C (90°F) heat that beats down on Pag and local town Novalja. Yep, the weather is a definite plus, as is the cost of accommodation, beer, and cigarettes—the fact everything is so cheap is another huge selling point.

Add to that the stupendous line-ups: Skrillex, Ben Klock, Ricardo Villalobos, Nina Kraviz, Soul Clap, Scuba, Seth Troxler, and Jamie Jones are just a few superstar DJs who have made the festival go off with

a bang. If that isn't enough, outside of Zrce Beach there is yet more party action with various boats casting off from the port of Novalja that host record-label led soirees to keep you dancing. If you're mad enough, you can literally get off your head for five days and nights straight, no problem!

The local mayor once joked that English pirates invaded Novalja centuries ago and that Hideout was the town's way of recouping the lost monies from that invasion! It must be said that Novalja has never seen anything like it: tens of thousands of Brits descend on the town, passing through its restaurants, bars, and clubs for an entire week. For some this would be like a living nightmare, but somehow the people of Novalja keep a smile on their faces as they encounter wave upon wave of wasted ravers. Must be something to do with all the cash that gets pumped into the local economy over the five days...

**DATE:** EARLY JULY

**PAST HEADLINERS:** CHASE & STATUS, SKREAM & BENGA, SBTRKT, MODESELEKTOR, RUDIMENTAL, LOCO DICE, ANDY C, CLAUDE VON STROKE, PENDULUM, EROL ALKAN, TENSNAKE, MARCO CAROLA, SHY FX

**TICKET PRICE:** ✪✪✪

**ACCOMMODATION:** ✪✪

**PRICE OF BEER:** ✪✪

**PRICE OF CIGARETTES:** ✪✪

**AVERAGE COST OF A SNACK AT THE FESTIVAL:** ✪✪

# I Love Techno

## GHENT, BELGIUM

Another Belgian festival (see, not as boring as everyone makes out!), this time with a name that basically tells you everything you need to know, well sort of... I Love Techno IS a techno-orientated festival but, like 10 Days Off (see page 46), the term is applied quite loosely, with acts playing styles of music that evolved from the Detroit-born genre. Touted as one of the biggest electronic music festivals in Europe, I Love Techno is held in Ghent, that most famous of techno meccas. Despite its humble location, the event is a massive deal and attracts superstars from all over the world, as well as plenty of eager ravers. And, while Ghent may not be well-known for its techno output, it certainly knows how to put on a party!

Belgians are the raving dark horses of Europe, and its many summer events are proof of this. Whether you love techno, drum 'n' bass, dubstep, electro, or any other genre that has been derived from techno, then this is worth a shout for sure.

Erol Alkan, Boyz Noise, Netsky, Sub Focus, Jamie XX, and plenty more electronic music luminaries are hired every year to get the fists pumping, the men pogoing, and the women doing pretty much the same. It's a winning formula that has kept ILT rolling for the last 18 years.

DATE: EARLY NOVEMBER

PAST HEADLINERS: TIGA, DJ FRESH, BOYS NOIZE, VITALIC, MAJOR LAZER, KNIFE PARTY, LEN FAKI, UNDERWORLD

TICKET PRICE: ✪✪✪✪

ACCOMMODATION: ✪✪✪

PRICE OF BEER: ✪✪✪

PRICE OF CIGARETTES: ✪✪

AVERAGE COST OF A SNACK AT THE FESTIVAL: ✪✪✪

DATE: AUGUST

PAST HEADLINERS: CARL COX,
SKRILLEX, MACEO PLEX,
ARMIN VAN BUUREN,
LUCIANO, DUBFIRE, FERRY
CORSTEN, SASHA

TICKET PRICE: ✪✪✪

ACCOMMODATION: ✪✪✪

PRICE OF BEER: ✪

PRICE OF CIGARETTES: ✪

AVERAGE COST OF A SNACK
AT THE FESTIVAL: ✪✪

# Kazantip

## UKRAINE

A festival that probably lasts longer than any other, Kazantip is a very unique event for many reasons, not least the fact that it runs for almost six weeks! One for the true diehards out there, Kazantip also boasts its own republic, complete with a president (Nikita, the owner), "Ministers," a private security team, and "citizens," i.e. us ravers. As if that wasn't enough, everyone is encouraged to wear orange, or carry yellow suitcases, or both. Obviously this makes the festival a very bright and colorful affair. During its twenty-year history, Kazantip's reputation for a good time has spread across Europe, although it still remains under the radar of many festival lovers.

A shame because many of those who have been say it's one of the best things they've ever done, even if they just dipped in for a weekend (which you can do, of course). President Nikita has two sayings: "Summer all year round" and "Life with no pants," which pretty much sums up Kazantip— a crazy place full of crazy party people, a crazy line-up of hundreds of DJs, and, get this, the Ukrainian police are not allowed in unless they enter as fully-fledged ravers. Sounds golden to me.

# Love System Festival

## PETRCANE, CROATIA

How many festivals can Croatia handle?! More than its fair share obviously, as it adds yet another British-born festival to its arsenal. The Love System Festival takes place in Petrcane, the beautiful location once occupied by the Garden Festival (see page 60), which has since moved on. Intimate, respectful of the local beauty, and curated by a team that has years and years of experience putting on parties across the UK, LSF also has the advantage of taking place early on in the season, bypassing the worry that it will be overrun by kids on their school holidays. The obligatory beach and boat parties are supplemented by a cool line-up, which includes Shonky, George FitzGerald, Ralph Lawson, Bicep, and Midland.

**DATE:** END OF MAY

**PAST HEADLINERS:** MARIO BASANOV, FINNEBASSAN, EJECA, JAY SHEPHEARD, LOVEBIRDS, CLAPTONE, SHIR KHAN

**TICKET PRICE:** ✪✪

**ACCOMMODATION:** ✪✪

**PRICE OF BEER:** ✪✪

**PRICE OF CIGARETTES:** ✪✪

**AVERAGE COST OF A SNACK AT THE FESTIVAL:** ✪✪

# Melt!

## GRÄFENHAINICHEN GERMANY

DATE: END OF JULY

PAST HEADLINERS: SOULWAX, BABYSHAMBLES, BLOC PARTY, ALT-J, LANA DEL REY, WHITEST BOY ALIVE, THE RAPTURE, MARCEL DETTMANN, M.A.N.D.Y.

TICKET PRICE: ✪✪✪

ACCOMMODATION: ✪✪✪

PRICE OF BEER: ✪✪✪

PRICE OF CIGARETTES: ✪✪✪

AVERAGE COST OF A SNACK AT THE FESTIVAL: ✪✪

A festival which lives up to its name in some respects, well… if you abuse yourself to the point at which your brain melts. This is another great German festival that takes place in an awesome location, Ferropolis AKA The City Of Iron, in Gräfenhainichen, a town just down the road from Dessau. Melt! has a sterling reputation — as most German festivals do — thanks to its exceptional organization and on-point musical programming, which the promoters themselves tout as "electronic meets rock."

Headliners have included Goldie and his ex Bjork (not together), Scissor Sisters, Editors, The Streets, and the magnificently named Wankelmut. The beauty of Melt! is also the location; the previously mentioned Ferropolis is a giant open-air museum full of old machinery from the mid-twentieth century. And when I say machinery, I'm not talking about old grandfather clocks; I mean giant, massive, huge old things that can weigh nearly 2,000 tons and stand 30 meters high. Insane.

# Motel Mozaique

## ROTTERDAM, HOLLAND

If you're a bit sick and tired of camping at festivals, then Motel Mozaique is THE alternative for you. Personally, I detest camping, it's something I have rarely done and, when I did, it was an absolute nightmare. At Bestival I spent a night in a tent that was almost blown away by a full-on gale, while at Standon Calling the temperature forced me to move from a tiny, freezing cold tent to the back of a van. No lie.

Motel Mozaique takes an obscure theme and runs away with it. It's all in the name... ravers are encouraged to stay in temporary art spaces/venues called "motels" that are curated by artists hired by the festival to entertain its guests. Cool, eh? These motels utilize numerous locations around Rotterdam and give visitors a completely unique and utterly unforgettable experience.

Now I may sound like a PR for the festival, but honestly, I dare anyone not to be enthusiastic about this. Even if you absolutely love your own bed and hate the thought of sleeping anywhere else, this is such a novel concept that you could at least suppress your concerns for one or two nights. Locations for the motels have included huts set up in trees, churches, shop windows, a construction site, and festival venues themselves. Imagine waking up to Mumford & Sons (a dream come true for some, or possibly a nightmare!), it can happen at Motel Mozaique. In fact, during the 2012 edition over 200 people enjoyed breakfast slap bang in the middle of Rotterdam's busy city center as part of the festivities. There's music, of course, there's art, and there's performance—a real treat and the kind of thing you'd only find in a country as open-minded and interesting as Holland.

**DATE:** EARLY APRIL

**PAST HEADLINERS:** TV ON THE RADIO, THE BLACK LIPS, DEUS, BELLE & SEBASTIAN, JOSÉ GONZÁLEZ, LYKKE LI

**TICKET PRICE:** ✪✪✪

**ACCOMMODATION:** ✪✪✪

**PRICE OF BEER:** ✪✪✪

**PRICE OF CIGARETTES:** ✪✪✪

**AVERAGE COST OF A SNACK AT THE FESTIVAL:** ✪✪✪

# Movement

## TURIN, ITALY

Held in Little Paris in Turin, the European incarnation of Detroit's lauded festival is a similar deal, but with a higher quota of Italians. The event came to life when owners Luigi Mazzoleni (Gigi) and Maurizio Vitale (Juni) got together with Derrick May and decided to adopt the event for their home nation. It started out in 2006 as a one-dayer and has grown and grown (and grown) into a beast of a festival, attracting huge crowds and taking over different parts of the city over the course of its duration, which is now almost a week!

DATE: END OF OCTOBER

PAST HEADLINERS: CARL CRAIG, JOHN DIGWEED, LIL' LOUIS, VISIONQUEST, DAMIAN LAZARUS, 2MANYDJS, CHRIS LIEBING, APOLLONIA

TICKET PRICE: ✪✪✪✪

ACCOMMODATION: ✪✪✪

PRICE OF BEER: ✪✪

PRICE OF CIGARETTES: ✪✪

AVERAGE COST OF A SNACK AT THE FESTIVAL: ✪✪✪

Being electronic-music based, the line-ups are fairly predictable—Seth Troxler, Laurent Garnier, Green Velvet, the Chemical Brothers, Richie Hawtin, Underworld, Luciano, Ricardo Villalobos have all played—but as these names are huge that's no bad thing and Movement try to avoid repeating the same name twice.

Having said that, the rest of the festival is anything but predictable. With parties taking place in a local car museum—Turin is the home of Fiat—the immense Olympic stadium, and along the banks of the River Po, you'll get to party in some pretty unique locations. Promoters Gigi and Juni love putting on events and have years of experience... it really shows. Plus who can resist the delights of Italian food? Unlike most festivals that leave you a few stone lighter, you're likely to need a winch to get you out of Turin after a week at Movement.

# Optimus Alive!

## LISBON, PORTUGAL

optimus
alive
Oeiras '13

It sounds like an episode of the eighties cartoon Transformers, but this is far from a battle between good and evil robots from outer space. Optimus Alive! is more concerned with music and arts and has quickly become one of the leading festivals of its kind in Portugal.

Reading through this book, you'll find that many festivals have grown in stature since their inception, a sure sign that there is an increasing global demand for such gatherings, and Optimus Alive! is no different. The festival's rapid growth in popularity has been pretty stratospheric and, in only its second year, it was named one of Europe's top parties. Several years later and the festival is going stronger than ever, each time assembling line-ups of epic proportions aimed squarely at trying to go one better than the previous year. Recent perfomers include La Roux, The XX, LCD Soundsystem, Crystal Castles, Calvin Harris, Pearl Jam, Metallica, Faith No More... need I say more? Seriously, Optimus Alive! is more than deserving of its apparently unnecessary exclamation mark. Shame there are no Decepticons, though.

DATE: MID-JULY

PAST HEADLINERS: RADIOHEAD, THE CURE, GREEN DAY, GRINDERMAN, DEPECHE MODE, PHOENIX

TICKET PRICE: ✪✪✪

ACCOMMODATION: ✪✪✪

PRICE OF BEER: ✪✪

PRICE OF CIGARETTES: ✪✪

AVERAGE COST OF A SNACK AT THE FESTIVAL: ✪✪

DATE: END OF AUGUST

PAST HEADLINERS: TALIB KWELI, SHY FX, THE PHARCYDE, LTJ BUKEM, CAPLETON, EZ, ZINC, LEE SRATCH PERRY

TICKET PRICE: ✪✪✪✪

ACCOMMODATION: ✪✪✪

PRICE OF BEER: ✪✪

PRICE OF CIGARETTES: ✪✪

AVERAGE COST OF A SNACK AT THE FESTIVAL: ✪✪✪

# Outlook

## PULA, CROATIA

Since its first appearance on the festival circuit in the mid-2000s, Croatia's seemingly endless list of parties continues to grow as the years go by. Pretty impressive when you think that up until recently it wasn't exactly a tourism hotspot and people would have struggled to name one festival there, let alone ten. Outlook is definitely one of the parties responsible for the massive increase of ravers heading to the Adriatic coast every summer. A festival based on bass, it features many of the world's biggest dubstep, and drum 'n' bass acts, plus reggae and dub soundsystems, who all gather at the awe-inspiring Fort Punta Cristo, a large fort located in the beautiful city of Pula, and the nearby beach.

The location really is perfect. Partying inside a fortress is pretty impressive, and dancing on the beach to the deepest dub pumping out of a proper soundsystem whilst stoned out of your mind is also an unforgettable experience. Some might say it's what the music was made for.

As mentioned on page 56, Outlook now also has a younger brother, Dimensions; its house and techno-orientated sibling. This gives you a good excuse to go back and visit. So the Outlook family now offers something for everyone musically, even your mum and dad. Or maybe not.

# Øya Festival

## OSLO, NORWAY

Norway is where Øya takes place, all the way up there in Scandinavia. Now, as many of you will be aware, Scandinavians like a drink or two — it's something to do with the bizarre 24 hours of daylight issues they have to deal with — so they know how to party. Being one of Norway's biggest festivals, it attracts ravers from neighboring countries Sweden, Denmark, and Finland — a heady mixture of Scandinavian party people, who can all devour their fair share of booze and party, Viking-style (without the raping and pillaging), for five days solid.

Øya started in 1999, and now stands strong as Norway's premier music festival, bringing thousands of people to Oslo's Medieval Park. It's the perfect location for a rave, with a picturesque fjord right next to it, Ekeberg Hill to the west, and there's even an eleventh-century church on the grounds. Acts that have appeared at Øya range from Björk and Yoko Ono to Morrissey and Vampire Weekend. In fact, Øya brings in over 80 awesome acts across its four stages (Enga, Sjøsiden, Vika and Klubben) during five days of madness.

DATE: EARLY AUGUST

PAST HEADLINERS: KANYE WEST, PULP, FLEET FOXES, BLUR, SLAYER, KRAFTWERK, WU-TANG CLAN, THE BLACK KEYS, AŞAP ROCKY, BEACH HOUSE, TAME IMPALA

TICKET PRICE: ✪✪✪

ACCOMMODATION: ✪✪✪✪

PRICE OF BEER: ✪✪✪✪

PRICE OF CIGARETTES: ✪✪✪✪

AVERAGE COST OF A SNACK AT THE FESTIVAL: ✪✪✪✪

# Positivus

## SALACGRĪVA, LATVIA

Latvia — not somewhere many of us have ever considered visiting, I presume? Maybe I'm wrong, but in comparison with Miami, New York, Sydney, or even London, I'm not sure Latvia is in many peoples' top ten places to visit. This is a real shame because it's a lovely place with a great little festival that's all about positivity. It takes place in Salacgrīva, an hour and a half 's drive outside the capital, Riga. Set in woodland next to the beach, Positivus is a quaint event which attracts tons of locals and the odd outsider, too.

The festival is relatively small, with around 25,000 visitors at last count. As a result it's never too hectic, which makes it perfect for families. Having a beach on site is great fun when it doesn't rain, which has been known to happen on occasion. Another bonus of the small size is there's little chance of losing your mates or missing your favorite act because you've had to trek for miles between stages. Headliners have included OK Go, Manic Street Preachers, Niki and The Dove, The Vaccines and plenty more great acts from across Europe and further afield. For a small festival, the line-ups are pretty diverse and, with sponsors like Red Bull involved, you're guaranteed a good quality of artist. It's also cheap, with a weekend ticket costing just €53. For something a little more relaxed and out of the way, this is ace.

**DATE:** THIRD WEEK OF JULY

**PAST HEADLINERS:** FRIENDLY FIRES, THE XX, CRYSTAL CASTLES, KEANE, SIGUR ROS, MUSE, MARK RONSON

**TICKET PRICE:** ✪✪✪

**ACCOMMODATION:** ✪✪✪

**PRICE OF BEER:** ✪✪

**PRICE OF CIGARETTES:** ✪✪

**AVERAGE COST OF A SNACK AT THE FESTIVAL:** ✪✪✪

# Primavera Sound

## BARCELONA, SPAIN

A precursor to Sonar (see page 82), but with less emphasis on dance music, Primavera Sound happens a month before Barcelona's "other festival" and features a wider variety of musical styles. Anyone who's been to Barcelona will understand what a fun place it is: cheap, sunny for most of the year, and picturesque, with great beaches and lots to do, making this the ideal spot for a few days away. It's even better when there's a festival on.

> DATE: LATE MAY
>
> PAST HEADLINERS: DAVID BYRNE, THE KNIFE, GRIZZLY BEAR, NICK CAVE, THE POSTAL SERVICE, ANIMAL COLLECTIVE, THE CURE
>
> TICKET PRICE: ✪✪✪
>
> ACCOMMODATION: ✪✪✪
>
> PRICE OF BEER: ✪✪
>
> PRICE OF CIGARETTES: ✪✪
>
> AVERAGE COST OF A SNACK AT THE FESTIVAL: ✪✪✪

Primavera is a three-day party and one of Spain's largest, with an annual attendance of around 100,000. Besides the eclectic line-ups, which include Blur, My Bloody Valentine, Sonic Youth, Hot Chip, James Blake, Iggy & The Stooges, and lots more, there's also a staunch focus on newcomers and showcasing what the Spanish music world has to offer. Though there's a lot of attention lavished upon Sonar, Primavera Sound is well worth a shout. Or you can put your raving endurance to the test by booking tickets for both and seeing how you fare. Go on, I double dare you!

# Pukkelpop

## KIEWIT, BELGIUM

Only a Belgian festival could have such a silly name! Pukkelpop is actually the country's second biggest festival (after Rock Werchter) and has been around since the mid-eighties, 1985 to be precise. Listing even a small number of the artists who've appeared there would be as silly as the festival's name, all you need to know is that the party is very, very big and includes lots of illustrious names, including Nirvana, Radiohead, Red Hot Chili Peppers, and Daft Punk.

England's very own Anne Clark, poet and songwriter, appeared on the bill at the very first Pukklepop along with six other acts. It was attended by 3,000 people and, according to reports, was a thoroughly enjoyable shindig. The festival today is completely unrecognizable from that initial gathering, having grown to host over 60,000 visitors each day, it moved location to the tiny village of Kiewit. Expect a mainly Belgian crowd, with the odd foreigner here and there; expect a huge array of music, great beer, and good times. You can also expect the odd bit of rain, too. Don't say we didn't warn you.

**DATE:** MID-AUGUST

**PAST HEADLINERS:** EMINEM, NINE INCH NAILS, SNOOP DOGG, FRANZ FERDINAND, ARCTIC MONKEYS, NEIL YOUNG, METALLICA

**TICKET PRICE:** ✪✪ (INCLUDES PUBLIC TRANSPORT COSTS)

**ACCOMMODATION:** (INCLUDED IN TICKET PRICE)

**PRICE OF BEER:** ✪✪

**PRICE OF CIGARETTES:** ✪✪

**AVERAGE COST OF A SNACK AT THE FESTIVAL:** ✪✪

# Rock En Seine

## SAINT-CLOUD, FRANCE

France! Land of baguettes, garlic, cheese, and wine... and lots more, of course. One thing that France never seems to be able to be very successful at is music, not on a global scale anyway. That may sound a little offensive to the French, but it is pretty true. Although they have some hugely talented artists that have seen success over the years (Daft Punk anyone?), there never seems to be a consistent flow of great acts from the Gauls. And who can name one French festival? Up until now, not many people. But that's about to change with this book, I'm hoping that the French festivals I mention in this book, all three of them, will soon be known by millions of festival-enthusiasts around the world. They deserve it.

Here's the first: Rock En Seine, a self-explanatory festival that takes place in Paris and is probably most famous outside of France for being the festival where Oasis finally split up. Aside from two Manc brothers deciding they don't want to talk to each other anymore, Rock En Seine's main attractions lie in a) the lovely and convenient location just a few miles west of Paris—the beautiful gardens of the Domaine National de Saint-Cloud (try saying that after a few Kronenbourgs); and b) the awesome rock and indie line-ups featuring all the scene's very best performers—from Rage Against the Machine to the Pixies, Faith No More, and the Klaxons. Despite the festival's name, the bill sometimes veers off-course to include people who aren't necessarily "rock," like Calvin Harris, Tricky, and Major Lazer. It's a fun festival with over 100,000 attendees over three days and, if you've never seen a Frenchman headbanging before, an essential stop-off.

**DATE:** END OF AUGUST

**PAST HEADLINERS:** PHOENIX, KENDRICK LAMAR, NINE INCH NAILS, ARCADE FIRE, CYPRUS HILL, R.E.M., THE HIVES, KASABIAN, INTERPOL, MASSIVE ATTACK, FOO FIGHTERS, MY CHEMICAL ROMANCE, SYSTEM OF A DOWN, EELS, BLINK-182, ARCTIC MONKEYS

**TICKET PRICE:** ✪✪✪

**ACCOMMODATION:** ✪✪✪

**PRICE OF BEER:** ✪✪

**PRICE OF CIGARETTES:** N/A

**AVERAGE COST OF A SNACK AT THE FESTIVAL:** ✪✪

# Roskilde Festival

## ROSKILDE, DENMARK

You don't hear a whole lot about Denmark's music scene, but Roskilde has global resonance thanks to its brilliant music policy and the fact that it's a non-profit organization supported by a tightly knit network of volunteers. It's been around since the early seventies and has built a sterling reputation, which gives the event plenty of clout when it comes to signing up some of the world's most prominent acts across multiple genres — from the mainstream (Coldplay, Red Hot Chili Peppers, Prince, Bob Dylan, Björk, R.E.M, Kings of Leon, Kanye West, Oasis), through to the lesser-known DJs and producers of the underground dance world (Toddla T, Yelawolf, M83, Addison Groove, Martyn).

**DATE:** LATE JUNE/EARLY JULY

**PAST HEADLINERS:** THE WHO, RIHANNA, JACK WHITE, BRUCE SPRINGSTEEN, METALLICA, IRON MAIDEN, RADIOHEAD, THE PRODIGY

**TICKET PRICE:** ✪✪✪

**ACCOMMODATION:** ✪

**PRICE OF BEER:** ✪✪✪

**PRICE OF CIGARETTES:** ✪✪✪

**AVERAGE COST OF A SNACK AT THE FESTIVAL:** ✪✪

Roskilde is one of the biggest festivals in Europe, with 80,000 weekend tickets sold, with an additional 30,000 volunteers, workers and performers boosting the capacity to 110,000. Like most festivals of its size, there have been a few negative incidents at Roskilde over the years, one of the most well-known coming when eight people tragically died in a crowd surge at the 2000 edition of the festival during a performance by Pearl Jam. However, the festival has continued and put that unfortunate incident behind it, remaining the jewel in the crown during Denmark's summer months and is most definitely an essential stop-off for anyone who has yet to experience partying Danish-style.

Denmark is not the cheapest country to visit, which means festival prices are expensive in comparison to some others in Europe, but the cracking atmosphere, beautiful crowd, and excellent line-ups make it well worth the cost. And if you're really short on cash, there are other ways to get in. One of the most (literally) eye-opening aspects of Roskilde is its annual Nude Run. The male and female winners of the race each get a ticket to the following year's festival for their efforts, so the skint amongst you should start training. There aren't many sights more amusing than naked men and women running for dear life with their floppy bits bouncing around and a look of pained embarrassment on their faces!

As I said, Roskilde is a non-profit organization, meaning all the profit made during the festival is donated to other humanitarian, non-profit, and cultural projects around the globe. A massive thumbs-up all round then... just make sure you've put in enough exercise for the Nude Run, so those floppy bits are a bit firmer.

# Snowbombing

## MAYRHOFEN, AUSTRIA

Combining two highly enjoyable pastimes — skiing and clubbing — Snowbombing is one of Europe's most popular festivals, taking place in the tiny Austrian mountain town Mayrhofen. Every April thousands of revelers descend on the resort to party for a whole week, taking in some of the world's best dance acts — from The Prodigy and Chase & Status to Dizzee Rascal, Example, and a host of more underground names such as Seth Troxler, Busy P, and Justin Martin. Though its line-ups are a focal point, Snowbombing has loads more to offer than just a huge amount of great music. For instance, the location alone is breathtaking. Imagine partying all night then waking up in the morning to a perfect view of snow-covered mountain peaks, a marked improvement on opening up your tent door to see a million other tents.

**DATE:** EARLY APRIL

**PAST HEADLINERS:** KASABIAN, ABOVE & BEYOND, CARL COX, HIGH CONTRAST, SNOOP DOGG, GROOVE ARMADA, DJ SHADOW, CHASE & STATUS, EXAMPLE

**TICKET PRICE:** ✪✪✪✪

**ACCOMMODATION:** ✪✪✪ TO ✪✪✪✪

**PRICE OF BEER:** ✪✪✪

**PRICE OF CIGARETTES:** ✪✪

**AVERAGE COST OF A SNACK AT THE FESTIVAL:** ✪✪✪

At Snowbombing fancy dress is par for the course, so expect to see people dressed up, both day and night, without fail. There is no theme, people just bring whatever they like and wear it. The fun and games start early, too. Whether the fresh mountain air is to blame has yet to be proven, but it seems that the recovery time for most Snowbombing revelers is a lot less than for the regular festivalgoer. Expect to see people falling over themselves first thing in the morning, as well as at night.

Being in the mountains also means there are ample opportunities to party in the kind of locations that you just can't find at any other festival. Jägermeister at the top of the whitest of white ski slopes? No problem. Fatboy Slim playing a set in an igloo? Done. Jamie Jones throwing down the deepest of deep house in a wooden shack? Yup!

Snowbombing makes sure the local environment is utilized to its full potential, with possibly the best parties happening in the nearby Eristoff Forest. In recent years both The Prodigy and Dizzee Rascal brought the house down in amongst the trees.

Aside from all the partying and great food (you have to eat a meat sandwich at Hans the Butchers, trust me), you must also try your hand at skiing or snowboarding while in Mayrhofen, a town famed for snow-based sports. The slopes are largely very good and the morning warm-ups are hosted by none other than aerobics legend Mr. Motivator!

Finally, if you consider yourself to be the archetypal intrepid festivalgoer, then there's an extra added bonus of the festival, which is the infamous road trip. Every year, 150 or so cars gather together in London before setting for Dover, crossing the English Channel, and heading over to Austria (via Frankfurt) on a wacky road trip. Smurfs, the Jamaican bobsleigh team, and superheroes are among the wide range of oddball teams competing in the road trip. Just make sure you pack a GPS with you, otherwise you'll end up lost for hours in a Frankfurt industrial estate like one unlucky duo in 2011!

# Sonar

## SPAIN

One of Spain's best known festivals celebrated its 20th anniversary in 2013, and deservedly so. In a country where festivals of all kinds occur on an almost weekly basis during the summer, Sonar stands strong as Spain's best electronic music and arts event. A day and night festival that aims to showcase the very best in electronic music, it features many of the world's most cutting-edge electronic acts.

It's not merely a DJ-led festival; there's always a variety of artists performing during the day and night segments of Sonar. All-important headliners over the years have included Trans Global Underground, Sven Vath, the mighty John Peel (RIP), David Morales, Guru (RIP), DJ Krush, Little Dragon, Yazoo, LCD Soundsystem, and an exhaustive list of many many more huge electronic acts, hip hop stars, and so on. Sonar is an event that changes the entire city; while the festival itself occupies a set space every year, there are many "Off Sonar" parties that take place across the Barcelona's many bars and clubs, which makes it an even more essential raving destination. Some of the amazing venues for parties have included Barcelona's spectacular W Hotel, Mac Arena Beach, and the lovely Poble Espanyol. It truly is a raver's paradise.

DATE: MID-JUNE

PAST HEADLINERS: KRAFTWERK, SKRILLEX, JURASSIC 5, PAUL KALKBRENNER, LAURENT GARNIER, 2MANYDJS

TICKET PRICE: ✪✪✪

ACCOMMODATION: ✪✪✪ TO ✪✪✪✪

PRICE OF BEER: ✪✪

PRICE OF CIGARETTES: ✪✪

AVERAGE COST OF A SNACK AT THE FESTIVAL: ✪✪

# Stop Making Sense

## TISNO, CROATIA

Another Croatian festival (don't say I didn't warn you!), Stop Making Sense takes place in Tisno — just like the Garden Festival (see page 60) — having started out in nearby Petrcane. Established in 2010, SMS has already become a very reputable event with strong links to some of the underground dance music world's most respected artists and record labels. Likewise, some of the UK's best-known promoters are fully involved with SMS — Secretsundaze, Warm, Electric Minds, Trouble Vision, and more — with each one assembling an all-star cast of the best musicians the underground has to offer. The crowd itself is pretty diverse and not just the typical collection of clubbers. You will also find a fair few curious holidaymakers who don't necessarily fit the typical "raver" mold, but instead appreciate a varied range of musical genres.

The location for Stop Making Sense is pretty special, a beautiful secluded bay and private beach that's made all the better by the top-notch weather. Party-wise, there's stuff happening during the day and night, with beach and boat parties while the sun shines and club nights once it has set.

Accommodationwise, you can camp a stone's throw from the main site or book a cheap local hotel. Either way it won't cost much to stay there. And if you're feeling flush, stay in one of the apartments or at the luxury boutique campsite set up by the promoters. Flights aren't too pricey either. As you may already be aware, beers are pretty cheap in Croatia and, with four days of musical anarchy to endure in the sun, you'll probably Stop Making Sense yourself by the end of the festival.

DATE: EARLY AUGUST

PAST HEADLINERS: RADIO SLAVE, SEBO K, PRINS THOMAS, LINDSTRØM, MOVE D, CHEZ DAMIER, DEETRON, STEFFI

TICKET PRICE: ✪✪✪

ACCOMMODATION: ✪✪✪

PRICE OF BEER: ✪✪

PRICE OF CIGARETTES: ✪✪

AVERAGE COST OF A SNACK AT THE FESTIVAL: ✪✪✪

# Tomorrowland

## BOOM, BELGIUM

This is what you might call Alice In Wonderland for adults. The kind of place where you could easily feel as though you're on an acid trip without even having taken the drug. Tomorrowland prides itself on its amazing stage set ups, with huge animated trees, rainbows, huge flowers that come to life, and lots more. It really is an enchanting environment to be in and one which creates a great atmosphere from the start. In this respect, Tomorrowland really has the upper hand over many of its rivals who, it seems, are happy to settle for relatively run-of-the-mill stages.

DATE: END OF JULY

PAST HEADLINERS: ARMIN VAN BUUREN, ABOVE & BEYOND, SEBASTIAN INGROSSO, TIESTO, FEDDE LE GRAND

TICKET PRICE: ✪✪✪✪

ACCOMMODATION: ✪✪✪

PRICE OF BEER: ✪✪

PRICE OF CIGARETTES: ✪✪

AVERAGE COST OF A SNACK AT THE FESTIVAL: ✪✪

But, of course, it's not all about the visuals, what really makes a festival great is the music and the people it attracts. Well, you'll be pleased to know that Tomorrowland also succeeds in both these areas. Music-wise it's aimed squarely at the commercial dance lovers out there; Afrojack, Steve Aoki, Swedish House Mafia, and the like have all made appearances, attracting absolutely huge crowds and courting controversy in the process. In, 2012 David Guetta was accused of "faking" his DJ performance, as video footage appeared to show that his volume faders were all down, but music was still playing through the speakers. Ouch.

Besides "fake" DJs and mind-boggling productions, Tomorrowland is another Belgian festival, which means great beer and good people. It takes place in a town called Boom, which I think pretty much says it all.

# Unsound

## POLAND

One of the primary aims of this book is to introduce people to new festivals and, likewise, to showcase events that really deserve your attention. Unsound is undoubtedly a festival that is worthy of a global audience, being slightly removed from the typical festival model and showcasing some really cool music-based projects. For instance, they once commissioned various electronic music luminaries to compose soundtracks to silent Andy Warhol films.

It originally started out as a purely Polish enterprise, but has evolved into a globally recognized event that pushes the boundaries of musical performance, often in parallel with visual arts. It's a very cool alternative to your standard muddy field affair. Not that it's trying to be different, Unsound just is what it is. There's no renegade attitude or blatant attempt to be alternative, it's just that there's such an abundance of samey stuff out there that, when someone does their own thing it stands out a little more.

Unsound's draw is the way in which it presents music in conjunction with installations, live performance, singing, and, most notably, unusual venues. Abandoned ballrooms, strange amphitheatres... anything but a standard festival stage, field, and burger van scenario goes. In fact, if it took place in London or New York, it would probably be full of chin-stroking musos. Fortunately (though a few members of the International Society for Chin-Strokers have passed through), there is still a large number of local Polish music lovers and artists who make up the overall attendance at Unsound.

DATE: END OF JULY

PAST HEADLINERS: SLAVA, SHED, ONEMAN, RON MORELLI, SHACKLETON, DUCKTAILS, ATOM™, RAIME

TICKET PRICE: ✪✪✪

ACCOMMODATION: ✪✪✪

PRICE OF BEER: ✪

PRICE OF CIGARETTES: ✪

AVERAGE COST OF A SNACK AT THE FESTIVAL: ✪✪✪

# Unknown

## ROVINJ, CROATIA

As everyone now knows by now, Croatia is an ideal festival location thanks to its super-hot summers, super-cheap booze and food and super-human humans. These three things combined with the right organizers — Manchester's Warehouse Project, Hideout (see page 62), and Field Day (see page 20) — make for something very special. It's clear that although Croatia is standard fare for festival goers, the location is heaven on earth. That combined with some very unique features — BoilerRoom.tv took over an island to broadcast live performances from the festival, for example — shows that the organizers are totally prepared to take the extra step needed to give ravers something fresh and exciting to get their teeth into.

Alongside the line-up that included Damian Lazarus, Richie Hawtin, Jessie Ware, Dixon, Geddes, Michael Mayer, Tim Sweeney, Jackmaster, and Joy Orbison, ravers discovered lots of weird and wonderful things around every corner. A walk through the nearby wood would reveal elaborate art installations or parties amongst the trees.

I was going to say "be prepared to step into the Unknown," but I won't. What I will say is, the whereabouts of your brain cells will be Unknown after a few days at this one!

DATE: MID-SEPTEMBER

PAST HEADLINERS: SCUBA, THE HORRORS, HENRIK SCHWARZ, MODERAT, JULIO BASHMORE

TICKET PRICE: ✪✪✪

ACCOMMODATION: ✪✪✪

PRICE OF BEER: ✪✪

PRICE OF CIGARETTES: ✪✪

AVERAGE COST OF A SNACK AT THE FESTIVAL: ✪✪

# Electric Elephant

## TISNO, CROATIA

With space for just 1,500 ravers, Electric Elephant is like a cozier version of Garden Festival (page 60), which is held in the same beautiful region. The benefits of having a smaller number of attendees — less crowding, a more intimate vibe, and a real sense of community — make this one of the go-to festivals for the more mature audience. Spending a few days at Electric Elephant means you soon get to know everyone else who's there, making the whole raving experience that much better. Likewise, the atmosphere is just as good for the DJs, and many choose to hang around after their sets to chat with audience members and generally have an awesome time — which is a huge bonus. And, of course, there are the boat parties, a staple of any Croatian festival.

In 2013, legends including Andrew Weatherall, Frankie Knuckles, and Radio Slave all turned in brilliant sets in front of a small number of very up-for-it party people. The general consensus from all who attended was that EE is one of the best festivals they'd been to in recent years, which bodes well for future editions. Where the name comes from is another story, but it's certainly a tag you won't forget in a hurry!

DATE: MID-JULY

PAST HEADLINERS: OPTIMO, CARL CRAIG, PROSUMER, MICHAEL MAYER, DERRICK CARTER, MR SCRUFF, JUAN MACLEAN, FRANCOIS K

TICKET PRICE: ✪✪✪✪

ACCOMMODATION: ✪✪✪

PRICE OF BEER: ✪✪

PRICE OF CIGARETTES: ✪✪

AVERAGE COST OF A SNACK AT THE FESTIVAL: ✪✪

# Weather Festival

## PARIS, FRANCE

A symbol of the growth of electronic music not only in France, but also globally, Weather Festival is a brand new gathering in the land of cheese and wine. Yep, they're popping up everywhere these events that revolve around massive line-ups featuring house and techno's demi-Gods and France is yet another country to have one of its own. No bad thing at all, especially when you find out that it's being organized by the people behind Paris' premier Sunday after-hours event, Concrete. Nina Kraviz, Marcel Dettmann, Raresh, Rhadoo, and Petre Inspirescu are among the names who played across three days at Weather's 2013 debut. On the Saturday 12,000 people packed into the Palais Des Congrès conference center to dance to local heros DJ Deep and D'Julz, while on Sunday the real hardcore carried on at boat parties down on the Seine that went on well into Monday morning. The atmosphere at all these events was considered to be electric by all who came down to party.

DATE: MID-MAY

PAST HEADLINERS: ROBERT HOOD, LEN FAKI, RPR SOUNDSYSTEM, BLAWAN, BEN UFO, KERRI CHANDLER, THEO PARRISH

TICKET PRICE: ✪✪✪

ACCOMMODATION: ✪✪✪

PRICE OF BEER: ✪✪✪

PRICE OF CIGARETTES: ✪✪

AVERAGE COST OF A SNACK AT THE FESTIVAL: ✪✪✪

# Worldwide Festival

## SÈTE, FRANCE AND LEYSIN, SWITZERLAND

Gilles Peterson is possibly one of the world's most respected selectors, at least in my eyes anyway. An ardent supporter of new music, regardless of genre, Gilles has established himself as a tastemaker who champions new talent from all over the globe. For many, his BBC 6 Music show is essential listening and his Worldwide Festival — based in the south of France — a popular destination for his many fans around the world who are up for some good fun in the sun.

Worldwide boasts a line-up curated by Gilles himself which, of course, is second to none, with DJ Marky, Tinariwen, Mala in Cuba, and Nôze all having played previously. But wait, there's a brand new addition to Gilles' annual knees up: Worldwide in the mountains! Yep, not satisfied with getting everyone out in sunny Sète, Gilles is now taking people up mountains to entertain them. Worldwide Leysin, a remarkable location in Switzerland, had its inaugural jump-off in early 2013 and is now an annual affair, just like its suntanned brother. So, it seems, whether you're a sunworshipper, snowbomber (see what I did there?), or just a fan of Gilles, Worldwide is where you want to be raving.

**DATE:** LATE MARCH (LEYSIN) AND EARLY JULY (SÈTE)

**PAST HEADLINERS:** NICOLAS JAAR, TODD TERJE, FOUR TET, FLOATING POINTS, MOUNT KIMBIE, PORTICO QUARTET, FLYING LOTUS, JAMES BLAKE, CUT CHEMIST, BENJI B, GILLES PETERSON, HUDSON MOHAWKE

**TICKET PRICE:** ✪✪✪

**ACCOMMODATION:** ✪✪ TO ✪✪✪

**PRICE OF BEER:** ✪✪✪

**PRICE OF CIGARETTES:** ✪✪

**AVERAGE COST OF A SNACK AT THE FESTIVAL:** ✪✪

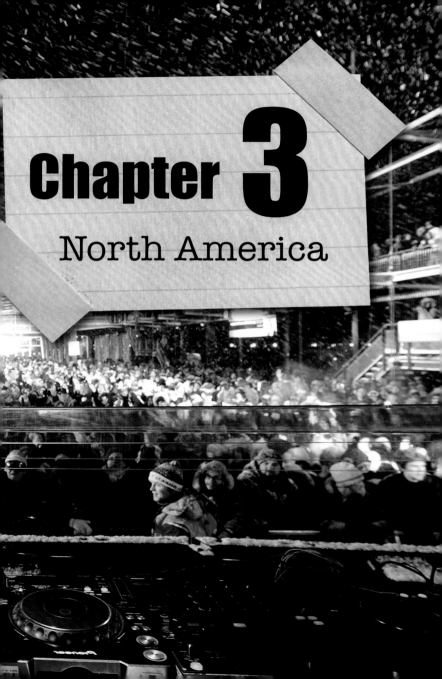

# Chapter **3**

## North America

# Art Basel

## MIAMI, FLORIDA

Miami knows how to party all year round, it's not just WMC and Ultra (see page 112) when the city's population get to let their hair down. Visit the city at any time of the year and you're guaranteed to find somewhere with an endless supply of booze and hot men and women to mingle with. Art Basel is a prime example of this — while it's primarily an art-based series of shows, there is plenty of music-related activity to get involved with while the artworks go on display all over the city.

DATE: EARLY DECEMBER

PAST HEADLINERS: NICOLAS JAAR, DANIEL JOHNSTON, SOLANGE, TALIB KWELI, GEORGE CLINTON

TICKET PRICE: ✪✪✪✪

ACCOMMODATION: ✪✪✪✪

PRICE OF BEER: ✪✪✪✪

PRICE OF CIGARETTES: ✪✪✪

AVERAGE COST OF A SNACK AT THE FESTIVAL: ✪✪✪

It's basically just an excuse for everyone in Miami to get even more wrecked than usual. So, while a large number of socialites and art lovers descend on South Beach, Wynwood, and various other parts of Miami, the raving fraternity also invade the city to see electronic music artists like Damian Lazarus and his Crosstown Rebels gang, hip hop stars Kool Keith and Rakim, and bands like Teengirl Fantasy and Thurston Moore of Sonic Youth fame. An eclectic selection of artists, which reflects the diversity of the crowds who attend the event.

# Bonnaroo

## MANCHESTER, TENNESSEE

For the uninitiated, Bonnaroo sounds like a pretty strange name for a festival — like an Australian party for kangaroos — but it actually means "to have a really good time." The event was named by rock bible *Rolling Stone* as one of the 50 Moments That Changed Rock 'n' Roll, creating a utopia for music fans across the US. The first Bonnaroo took place in 2002, where 70,000 people bought tickets to see Jack Johnson, Jurrassic 5, Blackalicious, and Ben Harper, amongst others. Since then the festival is widely regarded as one of America's best , each year winning plaudits for outstanding line-ups that have included Radiohead, Red Hot Chilli Peppers, Bruce Springsteen, Jay-Z, Stevie Wonder, and Bob Dylan.

The festival also has a policy of "Superjam Sessions," where often disparate artists are encouraged to perform together, like My Morning Jacket and R. Kelly and, really weirdly, Animal Collective and the guy who did sound effects in the Police Academy movies.

Locations have varied since its inception in 2002, but the Great Park in Manchester, Tennessee has recently become a more permanent home for the event, with 100,000 music fans making the pilgrimage there in 2012. This really is one not to miss.

DATE: MID-JUNE

PAST HEADLINERS: WILCO, PAUL MCCARTNEY, FEIST, THE ROOTS, THE SHINS, ALICE COOPER, R. KELLY, TOM PETTY, LIL WAYNE

TICKET PRICE: ✪✪✪✪

ACCOMMODATION: ✪✪✪

PRICE OF BEER: ✪✪✪

PRICE OF CIGARETTES: ✪✪✪

AVERAGE COST OF A SNACK AT THE FESTIVAL: ✪✪✪

# Burning Man

## BLACK ROCK CITY, NEVADA

Fast becoming one of the world's most notorious festivals, Burning Man shouldn't actually be classed as a festival in the traditional sense as it's more of a full-on life experience. It's a magical place where many "Burners," as they're known, come away with a completely different take on life, having been immersed in a world where money does not exist, community is a key priority, and there is no mobile phone reception. For seven whole days those who are lucky enough to get themselves an elusive ticket, and have the passion to organize themselves accordingly for the trip, experience just how great life really could be if the human race were to break free from the contraints of modern society.

In case you don't know, Burning Man has been in existence for around 25 years, starting out as a small gathering on Baker Beach, San Francisco in 1986. Just 20 people witnessed the first ever burning man ritual, where a wooden man is set alight and burned to the ground. It's a ceremony that signifies many different things for many different people and gave the event its name. In the years

since it has changed location to the extremes of the Black Rock Desert in Nevada, where a city is constructed for its week-long duration. The numbers have swelled from 20 back in '86 up to 50,000 in 2012 and the event is now attended by Burners from all over the globe—some new, some veterans, but all buying into the ideologies of the

event: making creative contributions to the community, taking all their own supplies, and joining everyone on an equal footing. There is no hierarchy at the festival, just a community of like-minded people all working together to make the experience the very best it can possibly be.

As one can imagine, spending a week out in the middle of the desert is no mean feat with the extreme conditions weighing heavy on even the most patient of people. By day it's very hot and at night the temperatures drop significantly. Add to that random dust storms and the fact that the alkaline sands in Black

DATE: END OF AUGUST

PAST HEADLINERS: N/A

TICKET PRICE: ✪✪✪✪✪

ACCOMMODATION: ✪✪✪✪✪

PRICE OF BEER: N/A

PRICE OF CIGARETTES: N/A

AVERAGE COST OF A SNACK AT THE FESTIVAL: N/A

Rock City can eat into one's skin if damp (as well as damaging metal and other materials) and you've got yourself some testing conditions, to put it mildly.

Travel around the city is pretty easy. Bring your own customized bikes or hop on to one of the many "art cars"—vehicles that have been embellished and enhanced by their creative owners. Accommodationwise, some people camp (mainly US residents), but many people travel to Burning Man in an RV/mobile home. Though it's not generally encouraged, an RV is a great place to take solace and, of course, get some respite.

However, to get the very best out of BM, you should really spend as much time out and about as you can, socializing, contributing to the community, and taking in all the amazing sights.

Music-wise, there's always stuff happening with bands, musicians, and some world famous DJs playing impromptu gigs at temporary "venues" across the whole of Black Rock... one of the most impressive is the Robot Heart sound system, a huge rig where luminaries such as Damian Lazarus and Art Department work their magic. Anyone who's seen the immense videos on YouTube will know what I'm talking about.

Being out in the desert means you pretty much have the freedom to do whatever you like. For the more narrow-minded observer this means sex, drugs, and rock 'n' roll, but there is a lot more to Burning Man than the average outsider thinks. Just take one look at all the amazing sculptures that are erected during the event, or the incredible sound systems, the creative classes, and all the other mind-boggling ventures set up by attendees during the week. Most amazing of all is

that Burning Man is a "leave no trace" endeavor. That means once it's all over, the organizers (and those who attend) take everything they brought along with them. No litter is allowed to be dropped or left behind and smokers even carry mini ashtrays with them so as not to flick their cigarette butts into the sand. The aim is to leave everything exactly how it was before the 50,000 attendees arrived. Incredible.

# Coachella

## INDIO, CALIFORNIA

Bearing very slight similarities to Burning Man, mainly because it also takes place in an American desert, Coachella has quickly become one of the go-to festivals for music lovers of all ages and plays host to a variety of genres. The crowd at the festival ranges from young teens who love a bit of weed, through to more mature music lovers. It's very much a bohemian festival at heart and very typical of California — sunkissed and hippified to the max. Prepare to witness plenty of stoned young folk chilling and swaying side-to-side to their favorite act (although with festival security super-tight you might have trouble tracking down a joint to smoke!). It is also a haven for celebrities, and if that's your thing you can attempt to seek out numerous TV and film "slebs" pogoing away in the crowd or, more typically, traipsing from one VIP area to another. Jessica Alba, Kirsten Dunst, Rihanna, Kate Moss, and more have all been pictured lapping up the good music and sunshine at the festival.

But Coachella has not become internationally known because of its famous visitors. It's much more to do with the ridiculous line-ups they pull in, with acts as diverse as Afrojack, Radiohead, and Snoop Dogg, who made headlines around the world at 2012's event when he performed alongside a hologram of the late Tupac. In one of the very first instances of hologram technology being used in such a way, Tupac was seemingly "resurrected" for the performance which left onlookers in awe and made the news all around the world. Not to mention the debut of Daft Punk's huge track Get Lucky in 2013.

Away from the music (and zombie holograms), Coachella is also an arts festival, which means there's an abundance of installation art to feast your eyes upon while walking around the site. You really will be gasping for a joint once you've come across some of the amazing creations that occupy various spaces around the festival site... art is (er... allegedly) always better appreciated whilst under the influence!

**DATE:** MID-APRIL

**PAST HEADLINERS:** THE BLACK KEYS, DAFT PUNK, DR DRE, LOU REED, THE POSTAL SERVICE, NICK CAVE, VAMPIRE WEEKEND, THE STROKES, KANYE WEST, ARCADE FIRE, MUMFORD & SONS, BEASTIE BOYS, PULP

**TICKET PRICE:** ✪✪✪✪

**ACCOMMODATION:** ✪✪✪

**PRICE OF BEER:** ✪✪✪

**PRICE OF CIGARETTES:** ✪✪✪

**AVERAGE COST OF A SNACK AT THE FESTIVAL:** ✪✪✪✪

# Electric Daisy Carnival

## VARIOUS CITIES ACROSS THE US AND BEYOND

Bearing similarities to the Ultra Festival (see page 112) in Miami, Electric Daisy is a traveling festival that in recent years has taken in US cities including Chicago, Las Vegas, New York, Dallas, and LA, plus Puerto Rico and London. The headliners at Electric Daisy are aimed squarely at the EDM crowd, so ravers into the more commercial end of the electronic music can expect to see artists like Swedish House Mafia, Kaskade, and Tiesto. But underground heads need not worry, more credible DJs such as Andy C, Cassy, and Justin Martin have also featured on the bill.

**DATE:** VARIES

**PAST HEADLINERS:** FERRY CORSTEN, MARTIN SOLVEIG, HEADHUNTERZ, AVICII, ATB, AFROJACK

**TICKET PRICE:** ✪✪✪✪

**ACCOMMODATION:** ✪✪✪✪

**PRICE OF BEER:** ✪✪✪✪

**PRICE OF CIGARETTES:** ✪✪✪✪

**AVERAGE COST OF A SNACK AT THE FESTIVAL:** ✪✪✪✪

Electric Daisy is also renowned for catering for the "table service" crowd: those who like to sit down in plush surroundings with a big bottle of posh vodka or champagne on their table. The clubbing "elite" if you will. It makes for a bizarre mix of Cristal-quaffing rich ravers and over-excited teens, which is about as entertaining as one can imagine. This may be off-putting to some, but it remains a monumentally popular festival. The 2012 Las Vegas edition attracted well over 300,000 people, and similarly huge numbers attended its other incarnations across the US, too. And whatever your opinion on crowds, just one look at the video footage from their events shows you just how much the revelers at their events love to party hard. The level of production on their stages is off the scale. An incredible amount of time, money, and energy goes into the light shows, glitter cannons, and pyrotechnics at Electric Daisy, which is just as much of a spectacle as the gurning EDMers and cork-popping VIP table dwellers!

# Lollapalooza

## CHICAGO, ILLINOIS

Chicago is the home of the "try pronouncing it when you're drunk" Lollapalooza Festival—an event that encompasses music, art, and performance. Of course, music is the main draw here with a wide variety of acts billed on the line-ups year after year. Kanye West? Done. Beastie Boys? Yup. Daft Punk, Ice-T, Depeche Mode, Arcade Fire, Pearl Jam…? All of those and more have performed at the festival, which prides itself on introducing its audiences to new talent as well as bringing in the more established artists. For the history buffs out there, the festival was started back in 1991 by Perry Farrell, lead singer of Jane's Addiction, as a farewell show for his band. But, as all great things do, it evolved into something much bigger and became a touring roadshow of sorts for up-and-coming musicians—like a traveling circus but without the freaks (or not, as the case may be)—before finally settling in Chicago's Grant Park in 2005.

Nowadays, Lollapalooza, which is just as difficult to write as it is to say, is much more than a music festival, incorporating a farmer's market and homemade arts and crafts stalls selling all manner of original items into its set up. Then there's the huge emphasis on recycling and the environment, with plenty of space for bike riders to park up. Which makes us all feel nice and warm and lovely inside doesn't it? Awwwwww, Wowapawooza… wuv wooooooo!

DATE: EARLY AUGUST

PAST HEADLINERS: THE KILLERS, THE CURE, NEW ORDER, THE NATIONAL, BLACK SABBATH, JACK WHITE, MGMT

TICKET PRICE: ✪✪✪

ACCOMMODATION: ✪✪✪

PRICE OF BEER: ✪✪✪

PRICE OF CIGARETTES: ✪✪✪

AVERAGE COST OF A SNACK AT THE FESTIVAL: ✪✪✪

# Igloofest

## MONTREAL, CANADA

Raving in sub-zero temperatures may not sound that appealing to begin with, and the name suggests you'll be spending a lot of time inside ice structures with eskimos BUT... Igloofest is one of the best parties you'll ever go to. For starters, despite the fact that it takes place in Montreal in winter (which means temperatures sink well below freezing), there's a special energy that emits from the crowd. The city's inhabitants are more than a little accustomed to the bitterly cold conditions and party just as hard as they would in the summertime. And Montreal itself is a cosmopolitan city of many delights, with a very welcoming, open-minded population.

> **DATE:** ACROSS FOUR WEEKENDS IN JANUARY AND FEBRUARY
>
> **PAST HEADLINERS:** A-TRAK, ADAM FREELAND, DJ SNEAK, MISS KITTEN, ELLEN ALLIEN, PAN-POT, TNGHT, MAGDA, AGORIA, AUDIOFLY , CHRIS LIEBING, TOMMY FOUR SEVE, JOY ORBISON
>
> **TICKET PRICE:** ✪✪✪
>
> **ACCOMMODATION:** ✪✪✪
>
> **PRICE OF BEER:** ✪✪✪
>
> **PRICE OF CIGARETTES:** ✪✪✪
>
> **AVERAGE COST OF A SNACK AT THE FESTIVAL:** ✪✪✪

Taking place at Montreal's Old Port, Igloofest is a month-long electronic music festival, which means a fair share of the world's best DJs and acts headline at the event. Buraka Som Sistema, Tiefschwarz, Maya Jane Coles, Josh Wink, Diplo, local hero Tiga, and many more artists—both established and upcoming—have been hired to inject some heat into the crowds at the festival.

And if the idea of partying as the snow falls around you wasn't enough, there's an ever present sense of fun that pervades at Igloofest—from the comedy hats everyone wears to its annual "one-piece" competition where visitors to the festival are encouraged to rock their most garish one-piece ski suits. The winners receive a coveted bundle of prizes usually containing VIP tickets to the following year's Igloofest and more, so people go to a lot of effort. Of course, they also acquire the kudos that comes with being the most badly-dressed person at the event... a title to be proud of!

# Montreal Jazz Festival

## MONTREAL, CANADA

You may be wondering why a jazz festival is included in a book about the world's best raves... well wonder no more as I'm going to explain exactly why this is an essential destination for any right-minded raver. You may expect this to be a series of sleep-inducing jazz gigs in small, smokey clubs around Montreal. However, the jazz festival is a huge occasion that attracts some of the world's best musicians, covering everything from blues, indie, soul, and jazz through to hip hop stars and DJs from the dance music world. It's a fantastic event that really showcases the diversity of jazz and its influences, and the forward-thinking nature of Montreal's people. For over a week, parts of the city's downtown area are closed off to traffic to allow for open-air concerts to take place in its streets... something that would be impossible to achieve in many other large cities around the world. Dispel any images of angry car-owners shaking their fists at drunken revelers; the city unites to share a love of music and good times.

The festival started in 1980 and, by 2004, had been named the World's Largest Jazz Festival by the Guinness Book of World Records. The figures speak for themselves, 650 concerts (450 of which take place outside), 3,000 artists from 30 countries, and a staggering 2.5 million visitors. Insane actually, especially when you consider that some of the concerts are attended by up to 200,000 people—more than the annual attendance of Glastonbury, at ONE single gig.

Due to its size, it's no surprise to learn past headliners have included legends like Aretha Franklin, Leonard Cohen, and Steely Dan— just a small indication of how many luminaries have appeared there alongside cutting-edge acts from the world over. This is another festival where the clientele ranges in age, background, and social status; you can find old, young, families, singletons, and everyone in between, all united by music and arts. The fact that it takes place in the summer is also a massive bonus—no freezing conditions at the Jazz fest (unless you're very unlucky!). So, make sure you line your stomach with plenty of meat sandwiches from the famous Schwartz's deli before you head out to the festival and overindulge. You won't regret it.

DATE: END OF JUNE

PAST HEADLINERS: ROBERT PLANT, RAY CHARLES, PAUL SIMON, JAMES TAYLOR, STEVIE WONDER

TICKET PRICE: ✪✪✪✪

ACCOMMODATION: ✪✪✪

PRICE OF BEER: ✪✪✪

PRICE OF CIGARETTES: ✪✪✪

AVERAGE COST OF A SNACK AT THE FESTIVAL: ✪✪✪

# Movement Detroit

## DETROIT

Set in Detroit, the birthplace of Techno, Movement Electronic Music Festival is one of America's seminal dance music festivals. It had its first run way back in 1994, when the United States played host to the World Cup football (soccer to Americans) tournament. It wasn't until six years later when the lady behind 1994's World Party, Carol Marvin, decided to launch another similar event, this time named the Detroit Electronic Music Festival, with second-generation Detroit techno legend Carl Craig brought in as artistic director. The first Movement was a huge success, with smiles on faces all round. Result!

**DATE:** END OF MAY

**PAST HEADLINERS:** JOSH WINK, KENNY LARKIN, DJ SNEAK, MOODYMANN, RICHIE HAWTIN, SETH TROXLER

**TICKET PRICE:** ☻☻☻

**ACCOMMODATION:** VARIES

**PRICE OF BEER:** ☻☻

**PRICE OF CIGARETTES:** ☻☻

**AVERAGE COST OF A SNACK AT THE FESTIVAL:** ☻☻

However, since then the festival has had its fair share of issues and controversies, particularly Carl Craig's court battle with Carol Marvin over alleged breach of contract and unfair dismissal. The event has also faced huge financial difficulties over the years, not least when techno godfather Derrick May took charge, and the City of Detroit took away funding for the party. As a result, Movement suffered massive losses and its future was placed in doubt on more than one occasion.

Nevertheless, it has survived the last 10 years and remains one of the world's most respected electronic music festivals, particularly as it's held in the Techno Mecca. Though the city may still be struggling with the fallout of its automotive industry, Detroit's people are a friendly and welcoming bunch, the city itself is very aesthetically pleasing and, who knows, you might even be able to catch Carl Craig showing off his roller-skating skills at one of his secret parties.

# Rock the Bells

## LOCATIONS VARY

Throughout this book there are cameo appearances from hip hop stars... Snoop, Missy Elliot, Tupac even! But there are no festivals dedicated 100% to hip hop... until now. With a name inspired by LL Cool J, Rock the Bells purports to represent the very best that the hip hop world has to offer, and it does a great job of assembling rap royalty from both now and back in the day. Like a few other festivals previously mentioned, Rock the Bells doesn't stay in one place. Instead it moves from one city to another but, unlike any other festival in this book, Rock the Bells is full-on hip hop and rap from beginning to end. Artists who have played include Bone Thugs 'n' Harmony, Method Man & Redman, Prodigy from Mobb Deep, Common, Nas, Jadakiss, Salt-n-Pepa, Wiz Khalifa, Dipset, Naughty By Nature, Immortal Technique... phew! And that's just from two days, and many of these acts come right after one another on the SAME BILL. This is not a list from a few select years at Rock the Bells, this is taken from one single weekend. Insane!

Needless to say, the crowd is a mix of rowdy young Americans from all walks of life: the middle class country boys, the diehard street kids, and everyone in between. The atmosphere is electric from the get-go, with a constant flow of energy from the stage to the crowd and back again. It must be said that seeing hip hop's elder statesmen (and women) shoulder to shoulder with its young stars, all on one stage, is something else and certainly makes Rock The Bells an essential destination for any self-respecting raver.

DATE: VARIES

PAST HEADLINERS: WU-TANG CLAN, BLACK HIPPY, E-40, JURASSIC 5, LAUREN HILL, ICE CUBE, CYPRESS HILL

TICKET PRICE: ✪✪✪

ACCOMMODATION: ✪✪✪

PRICE OF BEER: ✪✪✪✪

PRICE OF CIGARETTES: ✪✪✪✪

AVERAGE COST OF A SNACK AT THE FESTIVAL: ✪✪✪

# Roots Picnic

## PHILADELPHIA, PENNSYLVANIA

Hip hop legends The Roots are behind this annual festival which takes place in their hometown of Philadelphia. Now, being The Roots — that is, an open-minded collective of music lovers — the festival is not simply full of all their rapper mates, like some open mic contest. No sir, The Roots curate their line-ups masterfully with just as much band-based music as hippity-hoppity sorts. I love the Roots, their video for What They Do is an all-time favorite, so it's unsurprising to see the guys assembling a festival that features talents like Grimes alongside Naughty By Nature.

The Roots Picnic, held on the waterfront, AKA Penn's Landing, is an essential destination for any music lover who finds themselves close to Philly at the start of June. As many residents will tell you, the city is like New York's cooler brother, and has produced its fair share of stars over the years: Jazzy Jeff, Will Smith, Boyz II Men, Freeway and the late Lisa 'Left Eye' Lopes are all among the city's hip hop royalty, but The Roots remain their pride and joy. At a recent edition of the festival, the group played backing band for De La Soul while Rakim performed the Paid In Full LP in its entirety... yes, from beginning to end! And you thought a Tupac hologram at Coachella (see page 98) was amazing...

DATE: EARLY JUNE

PAST HEADLINERS: DJ PREMIER, A-TRAK, KID CUDI, MAJOR LAZER, NAS, WIZ KHALIFA, LITTLE DRAGON, JAMES MURPHY, ST VINCENT

TICKET PRICE: ✪✪✪

ACCOMMODATION: ✪✪✪

PRICE OF BEER: ✪✪✪

PRICE OF CIGARETTES: ✪✪✪

AVERAGE COST OF A SNACK AT THE FESTIVAL: ✪✪✪

# Woodsist

## BIG SUR, CALIFORNIA

DATE: END OF SEPTEMBER

PAST HEADLINERS: WOODS, FOXYGEN, SKYGREEN LEOPARDS, PEAKING LIGHTS

TICKET PRICE: ✪✪✪

ACCOMMODATION: ✪✪✪

PRICE OF BEER: ✪✪✪

PRICE OF CIGARETTES: ✪✪✪

AVERAGE COST OF A SNACK AT THE FESTIVAL: ✪✪✪

As we get older some of us yearn for smaller crowds, less annoying young people to bump into, and a general feeling of intimacy at festivals... well I do anyway! For any of you who are, like me, getting a bit long in the tooth for the larger festival then Woodsist is the place for you... the annual attendance is around 300, yes THREE HUNDRED. That means there's no queuing for the toilets, no worries about losing your mates in the crowd (unless you really are wasted beyond the point of no return) and, probably, the chance to hang out with your favorite band — or at least wave at the lead singer.

The festival's location is also a plus, held next to the Henry Miller Library on the edge of California's Redwoods... by the Big Sur. It's all band-based, with a fair few lesser-known but awesome bands doing their thing; they have included Real Estate, Thee Oh Sees, Woods, Fresh and Onlys, Ducktails, and White Fence. The festival is so small that the bands and their guests make up a sixth of the attendance figures! Let's hope it stays that way: all cute and 'ickle and alternative, like a Goth baby.

# SXSW

## AUSTIN, TEXAS

South by South West, or the snappier SXSW, is a multimedia-based event taking place in Austin, the bohemian capital of Texas, a state more commonly associated with gun-toting cowboys than musos in media glasses and scrawny software developers. Now strictly speaking it's not exactly a festival in the traditional sense, but you can certainly get as much from South by South West (musically) as you could from a "regular festival"... and lots more besides, thanks to various technology-related seminars that take place throughout the duration of the event. Very much somewhere you can really learn a lot about the future of online enterprises, technology, film, advertising, and lots lots more. But what about the parties?

DATE: MID-MARCH

PAST HEADLINERS: JOHNNY CASH, ARCTIC MONKEYS, BEST COAST, FEIST, ODD FUTURE, JAPANDROIDS, NICK CAVE, HAIM

TICKET PRICE: ✪✪✪✪

ACCOMMODATION: ✪✪✪✪

PRICE OF BEER: ✪✪✪

PRICE OF CIGARETTES: ✪✪✪

AVERAGE COST OF A SNACK AT THE FESTIVAL: ✪✪✪

Well, at South by South West you can expect to encounter a multitude of bands and performers from all over the world, playing music ranging from indie to Latin rock, electronic, reggae, rap, disco, and, predictably, "experimental." It's an amazing place to catch new bands, particularly from the UK and Europe as record labels fly over their new signings to perform showcases for US record execs and tastemakers. Many artists have broke big here (Amy Winehouse, anyone?), so if you're a hipster "I saw 'em before they were big" type then this is definitely the place for you.

Alongside the well over 2,000 freshly signed and unsigned bands looking to be discovered, huge names like Yeah, Yeah, Yeahs, The Flaming Lips, Dave Grohl, Prince, Bruce Springsteen, and Jack White also drop by to play, meaning there really is something for everyone.

The SXSW Film Festival has also grown in popularity in recent years, with independent film and documentary makers all showcasing their latest work. So if you're driving yourself slightly insane trying to cram in as much new music as possible, take a breather and catch a movie instead.

Austin itself is a place like no other, and likely to be not what you'd expect. It has a very strong arts and culture scene, which makes it a great location for SXSW, and it prides itself on being the self-styled "Live Music Capital of the World." Of course, if you want to hit a firing range you won't have much trouble finding one either! So you can shoot first, throw shapes later...

# Winter Music Conference and Ultra Music Festival

## MIAMI, FLORIDA

If you've never been to Miami before, then the annual Winter Music Conference is the perfect excuse to plan a holiday there. It's an amazing place that is home to super-human beings, the likes of which you will never have seen before in your life. There aren't many places on earth with such a high concentration of women and men of an unbelievably high caliber.

---

**DATE:** MID-MARCH

**PAST HEADLINERS:** CARL COX, TIGA, SWEDISH HOUSE MAFIA, REBOOT, FATBOY SLIM, AFROJACK, BOYS NOIZE, PAUL VAN DYK, DUBFIRE, DEADMAU5, KNIFE PARTY, RICHIE HAWTIN, FAITHLESS, LAIDBACK LUKE, TODD TERRY, CARL CRAIG, SETH TROXLER, JAMIE JONES, MAYA JANE COLES, JOSH WINK, JOHN DIGWEED, SVEN VATH, FOUR TET

**TICKET PRICE:** ✪✪✪ TO ✪✪✪✪✪

**ACCOMMODATION:** ✪✪✪✪✪

**PRICE OF BEER:** ✪✪✪✪

**PRICE OF CIGARETTES:** ✪✪✪✪

**AVERAGE COST OF A SNACK AT THE FESTIVAL:** ✪✪✪✪

---

Away from all that eye candy, there's the madness of South Beach, a hub for posers and party people. In this part of town during WMC almost every hotel and bar has electronic music blasting out from their doors and windows, suped-up cars rev their engines up and down the streets, crazy people from all over the globe are out in force, and the weather is second to none. It's the perfect place for a week-long party.

WMC itself is not so much a festival but a series of conferences for music industry figureheads to shoot the shit about all the goings-on within music. At least that's what they say, it's probably just an excuse for artists and execs to get some sunshine and escape the winter back home for a few days! Away from the conference itself, almost every DJ/record label worth their salt in the industry comes to town and throws associated parties. As previously mentioned, a lot of this goes on around South Beach, but a few events now take place off the beaten track in Downtown Miami, such as the famous Electric Pickle nightclub.

In the same week as WMC, the Ultra Music Festival takes place. Again, electronic music is the focus, but Ultra attracts more of an "EDM" crowd—that is, mainly young Americans who dress up in Day-Glo gear, love a bit of MDMA—or "Molly" as Madonna famously mentioned during her appearance at 2012's Ultra—and basically get out of their minds for the whole weekend. Which is fine if that's your bag! It's a huge event, with over 150,000 ravers dancing to their favorites including Fedde Le Grand, Nicky Romero, Crystal Castles, Kaskade, Hardwell, and Martin Solveig.

However, in 2013 Miami's city commissioners almost shut the party down after claiming the event's newly added second weekend of partying could be "disruptive to the local business community and area residents due to noise, nuisance behavior of festival goers, and gridlocked traffic." Clearly not big fans of EDM then!

# Chapter **4**

## Further Afield

# Afrikaburn

## TANKWA KAROO NATIONAL PARK, SOUTH AFRICA

The name says it all, this is a South African festival that takes inspiration from America's seminal Burning Man event (see page 94). Based on the same ideals, although a much smaller affair, Afrikaburn is a community-based festival where children, families, twenty-somethings, spiritual types, and everyone in between are welcome to join the proceedings. It's held in the beautiful Tankwa Karoo National Park, an area of semi-desert that's perfect for an escape away from the humdrum lifestyle many of us have to endure.

**DATE:** EARLY MAY

**PAST HEADLINERS:** N/A

**TICKET PRICE:** ✪✪✪

**ACCOMMODATION:** ✪✪

**PRICE OF BEER:** N/A

**PRICE OF CIGARETTES:** N/A

**AVERAGE COST OF A SNACK AT THE FESTIVAL:** N/A

Many of the creative enterprises you'll experience at Afrikaburn are based on the same things you'll find at Burning Man: camps and small communities, strange vehicles, sculptures, musical and artistic performances, photography, and a whole host of other mind-boggling creations can be found at Stonehenge Farm, where the event has taken place since the first edition in 2007. Despite its young age, Afrikaburn's reputation is already rock solid and it's certain to cultivate a very strong community, hopefully across much of Africa, just like the American incarnation has.

# BPM

## PLAYA DEL CARMEN, MEXICO

DATE: EARLY JANUARY

PAST HEADLINERS: SASHA, JOHN DIGWEED, DIXON, CARL COX, LUCIANO

TICKET PRICE: ✪✪✪✪

ACCOMMODATION: ✪✪✪✪

PRICE OF BEER: ✪✪✪

PRICE OF CIGARETTES: ✪✪✪

AVERAGE COST OF A SNACK AT THE FESTIVAL: ✪✪✪

Up until recently, Mexico never really got a look in as far as festivals were concerned. In fact, you would have been hard pushed to find anyone outside of Central America who could name ten Mexican DJs. However, nowadays it's home to a talented new generation of artists, and one of the world's fastest growing festivals, BPM. Anyone narrow-minded enough to think Mexico is still all big hats and Mariachi bands will get a serious wake-up call from this festival, which celebrated its sixth year in 2013. Set in the jaw-droppingly beautiful location of Playa del Carmen, BPM attracts DJs from all over the world for an epic ten days (and more) of partying.

The list of headliners is endless, from Damian Lazarus and the Crosstown Rebels gang, to Mr. C, Richie Hawtin, Lee Burridge, Guti, Steve Lawler, and everyone from the more "underground" side of dance music. Of course, plenty of local acts also make an appearance, including hot new names like The Climbers, Louie Fresco, Nobody Knows, Bastard Love, Balcazar & Sordo, and many more, all of whom proudly showcase the wealth of talent that Mexico currently has.

Parties take place day and night, meaning there's an almost non-stop festive atmosphere which, when combined with locations including ancient caves and plush beaches, make BPM an essential destination. Thankfully, its distance from Britain means that the "wideboy contingent" is relatively low, although its proximity to the US means there's a risk of the equivalent "douche contingent" of jocks and frat boys finding their way across the border. All in all though, crowds are fun, open-minded, and musically well educated, which means you can dance the night away without too much worry that you'll be encountering tequila-swigging numbskulls at every turn.

# Corona Capital

## MEXICO CITY, MEXICO

DATE: MID-OCTOBER

PAST HEADLINERS: TRAVIS, THE XX, ARCTIC MONKEYS, M.I.A. STEREOPHONICS

TICKET PRICE: 🍺🍺🍺

ACCOMMODATION: 🍺🍺🍺🍺

PRICE OF BEER: 🍺🍺

PRICE OF CIGARETTES: 🍺🍺

AVERAGE COST OF A SNACK AT THE FESTIVAL: 🍺🍺🍺

Here's a festival that will confuse your pretty little brains. Corona Capital is a Mexican festival that apparently longs to be British, hiring a cast of misfits from UK shores every year. Its support of acts that represent the sound of years gone by (and the sound of now) is surprising, yet warms the heart. With over 60,000 people in attendance — remember Mexico City is one of the largest cities in the world — it's pretty far from a "boutique" affair and brings in the big guns year after year. Franz Ferdinand, Snow Patrol, Suede, Portishead, all the very best bands groups the UK has to offer combined with locals and major stars from other regions, such as Major Lazer and Vampire Weekend.

I think it goes without saying that Mexicans love to party, HARD, so be prepared for an intense few days at Corona Capital. You will have to dig as deep as you can for as long as you can if you want try to keep up with them. There are four main stages, each occupied by a crowd that is full of energy and ready for action—with shirtless men bouncing away to their favorite bands and girls going just as crazy, but with shirts on (mostly)!

While you're in Mexico City please make sure you indulge in some culture, too. There's so much on offer, with art galleries, theaters, and museums aplenty, plus great food. Yes, I know this isn't a tourism guide but if you make the trip to Mexico City it's important to check out some of the amazing sights. It's not all tequila with worms in the bottle, jalapeños and tacos. Mexico is a cultural centre and you'd be a complete fool not to make the effort to soak up some of its delights (yes, this book can be serious, too).

# Inti Fest

## LIMA, PERU

Apparently, the Inti Raymi ("Festival of the Sun") was a religious ceremony of the ancient Inca Empire held in honor the god Inti, who was one of the most venerated deities in Inca religion. Today's festival is a little less serious, in the religious respect at least. Instead, it is based on the notion that, in past centuries, Peruvians used music to elevate their spirits — as we all do — and incorporated music, dance, and rhythm into rituals where they connected their consciousness with the earth and nature. Whether this occurs at Inti is up for discussion, but what's clear is that they manage to curate some very impressive line-ups year on year with a direct focus on good-quality contemporary electronic music.

Like many similar events, it mixes up old and new performers to create a dazzling selection of musicians and artists, all of whom unite under the "underground dance" banner. You'll find no Guettas or Aviciis here! Adultnapper, Lee Burridge, Clive Henry, Bill Patrick, Geddes, and Jay Haze were among those who performed at the 2013 festival. The location, as one might expect, is pretty impressive taking place on Asia Beach, one of the country's many beautiful and popular stretches of sand. Being next to the sea adds to the "back to earth" feel the festival organizers like to promote.

Probably not somewhere that everyone will fancy visiting; it's not the most convenient location. But if you happen to be in the area on a backpacking trip, or want to sample raving in an exotic South American location, it's certainly worth heading to.

DATE: MID-FEBRUARY

PAST HEADLINERS: JOSH WINK, GUY GERBER, MARC HOULE, SOUL CLAP

TICKET PRICE: ✪✪✪✪

ACCOMMODATION: ✪✪✪

PRICE OF BEER: ✪✪

PRICE OF CIGARETTES: ✪✪

AVERAGE COST OF A SNACK AT THE FESTIVAL: ✪✪

# INTRO

## BEIJING, CHINA

Billed as "China's only electronic music festival," INTRO takes place in Beijing and most likely lives up to that claim. INTRO, which stands for "Ideas Need To Reach Out," has been around for four years now, with 10,000 people attending the first festival. Since then, INTRO has enjoyed a 50% year-on-year growth in ticket sales. Pretty good going considering the event's relative infancy and taking into account the fact China is not very well known for having a strong electronic music scene. The party is a city-wide series of concerts, art exhibitions, and forums, all based around electronic music — from techno and house to drum 'n' bass — and it manages to attract artists from around the world to perform alongside the local talent.

DATE: END OF MAY

PAST HEADLINERS: ROBAG WRUHME, OXIA, DOP, JOSH WINK, DIGITAL 21, CAD 73, PATRICK YU, PAK, SHENYUE, LUDO V, KENNETH C

TICKET PRICE: ✪✪✪

ACCOMMODATION: ✪✪✪✪

PRICE OF BEER: ✪✪✪✪

PRICE OF CIGARETTES: ✪✪✪

AVERAGE COST OF A SNACK AT THE FESTIVAL: ✪✪✪

INTRO is the brainchild of Miao Wong, head of Acupuncture Records, a China-based label specializing in house and techno. Having set up the whole event in 2009, he has worked tirelessly ever since to maintain the high standards set by the first outing. In 2012 Gui Boratto, Christian Smith, and Anthony Collins headlined the event, alongside Oriental stars such as Mickey Zhang, Ocean Lam, Kenneth C, and Mu Xiaohu.

As you may expect, the location for INTRO is rather industrial and stark. D-Park Plaza in the Chaoyang District of Beijing is surrounded by power plants and is touted as one of the last truly "Bauhaus-esque" locations in the city. For this reason, it fits perfectly with the music, offering a futuristic utopia with its smoke-spewing chimneys and metallic pipes. D-Park Plaza is located in one of Beijing's cultural and arts centers, so, of course, the clientele are all of a bohemian persuasion,

putting it on a par with many of the other festivals that take place around the globe. Expect to see a variety of nationalities present too, just a quick glance at the photos from the most recent event and it's possible to see westerners dancing side-by-side with those from China and the surrounding nations. INTRO has quickly become a focal point for the Far East's electronic music community thanks to its forward-thinking ideals and the way in which it lends a huge amount of support to local artists, who are sadly overlooked on a global scale.

As China becomes increasingly westernized, we can expect to see more festivals in the INTRO mold, bringing together different cultures and musical forms and encouraging the new generation of Chinese people to do the same. Much has changed in the east over the last couple of decades and events like this are proof that music festivals are yet another western pastime that the Chinese have warmed to. Needless to say though, as long as INTRO remains their only electronic music festival, it will remain an essential ticket for anyone wanting a taste of festivals promoted Chinese-style.

# Labyrinth

## NAEBA GREENLAND, JAPAN

One of Japan's best kept secrets (apologies to the organizers for putting it in my book!), Labyrinth is an out and out techno festival. Unapologetic in its selection of artists, the event takes place at an amazing location in the Naeba Greenland area of Tokyo. It's an open-air festival that has had "life-changing" effects on many of those who've been lucky enough to visit. It has a very stringent policy in terms of sound, relying heavily on the high quality Funktion One rigs set up around the stage. Somehow, the positioning of the speaker stacks works well with the surrounding woodland and there is minimal loss of sound strength and quality from night to day, meaning the techno gods who've performed in the past — Mathew Jonson, Shed, Peter Van Hoesen, Donato Dozzy and Move D are just a few — have all sounded as good as ever.

DATE: MID-SEPTEMBER

PAST HEADLINERS: FRED P, STEFFI, APPLEBLIM, STEFFI, FUNCTION, TOBIAS, SCUBA, SHACKLETON, MARCEL FENGLER, DJ SO

TICKET PRICE: ✪✪✪✪✪

ACCOMMODATION: ✪✪✪✪✪

PRICE OF BEER: ✪✪✪✪✪

PRICE OF CIGARETTES: ✪✪✪✪

AVERAGE COST OF A SNACK AT THE FESTIVAL: ✪✪✪✪

Labyrinth started out off the back of the once huge psy-trance scene in Tokyo. Of course, as often happens, the genre's popularity (which still mystifies me to this day) waned and techno took center stage. Though the often relentless genre may not seem that fitting to such beautiful surroundings, it continues to be the festival's music of choice and, whether it's soft and melodic or tough and imposing, the Labyrinth faithful lap it up.

As I've said, the beauty of Labyrinth's setting is a major part of why this festival is so special: natural woodland, rows of teepees and, most importantly, a welcoming crowd. Ravers in Japan are generally very serious about their music, but are equally into having fun... which makes for a perfect combination. It may be a Labyrinth but there's very little risk of finding David Bowie playing psy trance there, which makes it all the more enticing!

# Rainbow Serpent

## LEXTON, VICTORIA, AUSTRALIA

Something which is a little more of the typical festival mold, Rainbow Serpent takes place in western Victoria and encapsulates all that is wholesome and pure about festivals. It represents the very foundations of the festival model, that is: community, self-expression, arts, crafts, creativity, and respect for one another and the planet. For the judgmental it might seem a little too "crusty" or hippified, but for most it's a welcome change from all the corporate enterprises masquerading as festivals that we've become used to. As well as the electronic music aspect, which is always on point may I add, Rainbow Serpent offers health and healing experiences and even the name itself is related to an aboriginal "Dreamtime" tale.

DATE: AUSTRALIA DAY WEEKEND IN JANUARY

PAST HEADLINERS: SASHA, HARDFLOOR, GRIFF, OLIVER KOLETZKI, PROMETHEUS, GUY J, INTERPULSE, JONNY MAX, MALPHEMIST

TICKET PRICE: ✪✪✪

ACCOMMODATION: ✪✪✪

PRICE OF BEER: ✪✪

PRICE OF CIGARETTES: ✪✪✪

AVERAGE COST OF A SNACK AT THE FESTIVAL: ✪✪✪

In fact, the festival maintains strong ties with the aborigines, Australia's original indigenous population, which is possibly what I like about it the most. Ten thousand people agree, and it's built up a loyal collection of followers who return each year, giving it a very strong communal feel. If you want an alternative to all the bold, brash festivals that are currently occupying the world stage then Rainbow Serpent is well worth a visit. It is raving for those who represent the true ideals of raving.

# Soundwave

## VARIOUS CITIES ACROSS AUSTRALIA

This is rock 'n' roll done Aussie style, which means no holds barred action, a down to earth yet riotous atmosphere, and enough beer to fill up the Sydney Harbour twice over. Like its Aussie brother Stereosonic (see opposite), Soundwave is a traveling event and visits all of Australia's major cities — Perth, Melbourne, Adelaide, Sydney, and Brisbane — but unlike Stereosonic, with its focus on EDM, Soundwave is a festival dedicated to rock, metal, and punk, so be careful not to mix them up. Fluoro shirts, glowsticks, and brightly colored beads are going to make you stand out like a sore thumb when surrounded by thousands of black-clad metalheads ready to cut loose.

It all happens during February and March, when temperatures are at their highest (as someone living in the Northern Hemisphere, this still seems wrong!). The weather means that things can become pretty hot and sweaty at Soundwave, so carnage ensues wherever it touches down at a new city. All that jumping around and beer guzzling is bound to put more than a few people out of the game. Which makes for an interesting experience and one which sorts the men from the boys.

DATE: LATE FEBRUARY AND EARLY MARCH

PAST HEADLINERS: BLINK-182, LINKIN PARK, SLAYER, IRON MAIDEN, SLIPKNOT, SYSTEM OF A DOWN, GARBAGE, THE OFFSPRING, CYPRESS HILL

TICKET PRICE: ⬤⬤⬤⬤

ACCOMMODATION: ⬤⬤⬤

PRICE OF BEER: ⬤⬤⬤

PRICE OF CIGARETTES: ⬤⬤⬤⬤

AVERAGE COST OF A SNACK AT THE FESTIVAL: ⬤⬤⬤⬤

The headliners are all suitably tattooed up, headbanger-friendly bands including Anthrax, Metallica, Bullet For My Valentine, Paramore and, my faves, homegrown thrashers Amity Affliction. Soundwave's awesome line-ups and distinctly Aussie atmosphere creates an ideal raving hub, whether you're a rock fan or not. You just have to make sure that you're fully prepared for extreme temperatures and even more extreme rock fanatics.

# Stereosonic

## VARIOUS CITIES ACROSS AUSTRALIA

Another Aussie festival beginning with S that sets up in five of the country's major cities, but this is the electronic music alternative. Artists include Diplo, Tiesto, Mr. Oizo... basically anyone whose name ends in an O, and lots more, like Example, Caspa, Adam Beyer, Carl Cox, Laidback Luke, Loco Dice, Sub Focus, Kaskade, Ferry Corsten, and so on. It's a huge deal across Australia and draws in just as many people as Soundwave.

Although it's only been around since 2007, Stereosonic is already one of Australia's biggest festivals and its growth is incredible. In fact, it made headlines in 2011 when it was reported to have become the nation's biggest ever festival with 60,000 eager ravers attending the Sydney leg. It also won the award for Australia's best festival, that's not a bad year's work.

Just like Soundwave, Stereosonic has a fantastic party atmosphere. Aussies—both male and female—certainly know how to let their hair down and can consume a fair amount of booze, which makes for a hedonistic atmosphere and a constant supply of entertainment, both on stage and off it. Just make sure you keep your shirt on, the organizers have in the past tried (and often failed) to promote a "tops on" policy in the past.

DATE: LATE NOVEMBER AND EARLY DECEMBER

PAST HEADLINERS: CALVIN HARRIS, AVICII, CARL COX, MAJOR LAZER, LMFAO

TICKET PRICE: ✪✪✪✪

ACCOMMODATION: ✪✪✪✪

PRICE OF BEER: ✪✪✪

PRICE OF CIGARETTES: ✪✪✪✪

AVERAGE COST OF A SNACK AT THE FESTIVAL: ✪✪✪✪

# Together

## BANGKOK, THAILAND

Who'd have thought that anything in Thailand could do battle with the Full Moon parties?! Well, here's the proof, the Together Festival not only attracted well over 10,000 people in both 2012 and 2013 but also saw headline performances from none other than Snoop Dogg, Lil Jon, Justice, and Afrojack. A huge deal, but I guess unsurprising since there is such an abundance of well-off tourists in Thailand, as well as locals who want to have a good time. Bangkok is the perfect place for something like Together and the party has benefitted from its huge line-ups and the support from a country that really loves to party.

DATE: MID-JANUARY

PAST HEADLINERS: LMFAO, AFROJACK, SNOOP DOGG, AN21 & MAX VANGELI

TICKET PRICE: ✪✪✪✪

ACCOMMODATION: ✪✪ TO ✪✪✪✪✪

PRICE OF BEER: ✪✪

PRICE OF CIGARETTES: ✪

AVERAGE COST OF A SNACK AT THE FESTIVAL: ✪✪✪

One thing you've got to love about Together is its inclusion of local talent, something which, as I've said before, many festivals around the world sadly neglect. The addition of Thaitanium, a popular Thai hip hop group, Bangkok Invaders, and Superzaaap help to shine the light on the country's very own homegrown musicians.

Thailand is such a popular destination for so many travellers around the world that you can expect to meet people from a host of different countries at Together, which adds to the great atmosphere. Not to mention the cheap booze, cigarettes, and excellent weather. And, if you're partial to the odd ladyboy, then I'm sure you can stop off at the infamous Patpong district post-festival for a happy ending...

# Zoukout

## SINGAPORE

It's sometimes hard to believe that, even in an ever-shrinking world, dance music culture could have spread to shores as far afield as Asia, yet here's proof that what started in Chicago and Detroit can be successfully transported to a completely different culture. It's a beautiful thing. Some might say it's a homogenization of the world's cultures but I'm sure that, outside of Zoukout, Singapore is still pretty staunch in its local traditions. Maybe this is a subject that's a bit too big for a book that's simply about the world's best festivals, but personally, I'd say it can only be a good thing that music translates so well around the globe and inspires and unites so many people.

At Zoukout, which is overseen by the owners of Singapore's Zouk club, the emphasis is on dance music; cool, underground dance music with DJs like Seth Troxler, Maceo Plex, and Nina Kraviz featured alongside the festival-friendly bigger names like Hardwell and Above & Beyond. It's a very considered assembly of performers, with organizers ensuring they don't ostracize any particular groups of music lovers. By making it open to all, the festival experience is much better, with larger attendance figures and happy ravers all round.

DATE: EARKY DECEMBER

PAST HEADLINERS: KASKADE, PAUL VAN DYK, A-TRAK, PAUL KALKBRENNER, CALVIN HARRIS, BOOKA SHADE

TICKET PRICE: ✪✪✪

ACCOMMODATION: ✪✪✪✪

PRICE OF BEER: ✪✪

PRICE OF CIGARETTES: ✪✪✪

AVERAGE COST OF A SNACK AT THE FESTIVAL: ✪✪✪

Another benefit of Zoukout is that it's a beach-based event; being able to dance on the sand next to the sea makes it even more appealing. Raving in Singapore might seem like an alien concept to some, while others—those open to new cultures and experiences—will relish the opportunity to party with nearly 30,000 other ravers in a setting that's very different from the standard "stage in a field" festival.

# Index